Levels of Corporate Globalization

.

Levels of Corporate Globalization

Developing a Measurement Scale for Global Customer Management

Petra Kuchinka
Assistant Professor, Johannes Kepler University, Austria

First published 2004 by
PALGRAVE MACMILLAN
Houndmills, Basingstoke, Hampshire RG21 6XS and
175 Fifth Avenue, New York, N.Y. 10010
Companies and representatives throughout the world

PALGRAVE MACMILLAN is the global academic imprint of the Palgrave Macmillan division of St Martin's Press, LLC and of Palgrave Macmillan Ltd. Macmillan® is a registered trademark in the United States, United Kingdom and other countries. Palgrave is a registered trademark in the European Union and other countries.

ISBN 1–4039–3625–0

This book is printed on paper suitable for recycling and made from fully managed and sustained forest sources.

A catalogue record for this book is available from the British Library.

Library of Congress Cataloging-in-Publication Data
Kuchinka, Petra, 1976–
    Levels of corporate globalization : developing a measurement
    scale for global customer management / Petra Kuchinka.
        p.   cm.
    Includes bibliographical references and index.
    ISBN 1–4039–3625–0 (cloth)
    1. Relationship marketing—Mathematical models.   2. Customer
    relations—Management—Mathematical models.   3. Globalization—
    Economic aspects—Mathematical models.   4. International business
    enterprises—Management—Mathematical models.   I. Title.
    HF5415.55.K83 2004
    658.8'4—dc22   2003064656

10   9   8   7   6   5   4   3   2   1
13   12   11   10   09   08   07   06   05   04

Printed and bound in Great Britain by
Antony Rowe Ltd, Chippenham and Eastbourne

Contents

List of Tables and Figures

Tables

Figures

Foreword

Globalization has as many facets as the perspectives of the different scientific disciplines that deal with it. It is also true that it has become the centre of political, societal and managerial debates all over the world. The more that nations are faced with the good and evil outcomes of dynamics which are partly autonomous and partly induced by transnational companies, the more that managerial science has to deal with the implications on decision-making in companies, besides other developments which impede or accelerate the transformation of industries and business.

Dr Kuchinka's dissertation, which was written at the Department of Marketing at the Johannes Kepler University, focuses on the measurement of the level of corporate globalization (LoCG) as a marketing problem. From the marketing point of view, the issue of globalization is mostly addressed in the field of global marketing and key account management. The value of the dissertation is based on the theoretical framework developed and the appropriate measurement concept, which gives new insights into global key-account management. The developed model is further empirically tested by a representative sample of globally operating companies, Austrian and German. Readers of both academia and practice will draw their own useful conclusions from the research findings. For that reason, I wish the text every attention and success.

GERHARD A. WÜHRER
Chair and Head of Department of Marketing
Faculty of Business, Economics and Social Sciences
Johannes Kepler University, Linz, Austria

Preface

A rising level of globalization, in the sense of rising internationalization and globalization, affects not only the business world but, to a considerable extent, also the whole economic, political-legal, social and cultural environment. In fact, it is a phenomenon people cannot avoid and one that provokes two conflicting mental attitudes. For some people and companies it creates anxiety and uncertainty, which manifest themselves in major aversions to such development. For others, these developments create new challenges, chances and also risks. But a generally positive attitude towards rising globalization enables people and companies to adapt to changes over time. A 'prevention' of this phenomenon from today's viewpoint is not realistic. Therefore, it is necessary to cope with it – especially from a scientific viewpoint – and this fact constitutes the reason why the author was highly interested and personally involved in this research. According to the author's opinion, the task of science is the exploration and explanation of environmental developments with the objective of communicating with people and companies to reduce anxiety and uncertainty.

This research aims to contribute to this objective by answering the central questions of which dimensions characterize companies' different degrees of globlization, and how these dimensions can be measured in order to classify companies.

I would like to express my thanks to my first supervisor, Prof. Dr Gerhard A. Wührer, who supported me with professional advice, a readiness to discuss and personal free space, giving the chance to tackle the research problem intensively. I also gratefully acknowledge the help of Prof. Dr Lars Hakanson, my second supervisor, who always enriched research discussions with his professional competence in international management, an essential completion of my marketing perspective, as well as with his personal commitment.

Furthermore, I would like to thank Dr Atul Parvatiyar from Georgia State University, Atlanta for his support, as well as all my colleagues from the Marketing Department at the Johannes Kepler University, Linz. Last but not least, I would like to thank my family and my partner, Martin, for their encouragement, which helped me in difficult stages of my research to follow up my objectives and intention.

The author and publishers thank the following publishers and individuals for permission to reprint copyright material: Harvard Business School Publishing Corporation; Marketing ZFP, Vahlen; Atul Parvatiyar; D.J. Lecraw, A.J. Morrison and J.H. Dunning, and Routledge; Sales Profi; Fachverlagsgruppe Bertelsmann-Springer; Springer.

Linz   PETRA KUCHINKA

'...*absolutely no one who wants to understand our prospects at the century's end can ignore it [globalization].*'

(Giddens, *Runaway World*, 1999, p. 7)

1
Introduction

Globalization has become a keyword in many disciplines and in cultures worldwide. It is a trend that to some seems to offer unlimited opportunities, but to others invokes fear of loss of national identities, erosion of social systems, environmental degradation, loss of employment or loss of national sovereignty. Several different theses have arisen around the dichotomy of enthusiasm versus fear and exasperation. For one group of people, globalization is 'here to stay' (the 'globalist thesis'), for others globalization does not exist (the 'sceptical thesis'), for the third group it does exist, but it is more complex than assumed (the 'transformational thesis') and the fourth group accepts globalization as a phenomenon, but does not like it (the 'anti-globalist thesis') (cf. Kirkbride, Pinnington and Ward, 2001, pp. 18ff.).

One cannot deny that both positive and negative consequences of globalization exist. However, it is a fact that globalization is increasing and markets, companies and people must adapt. The question arises as to whether a coherent definition of globalization can be found that can build a basis for understanding, because only then can corporate globalization be operationalized and measured.

Measurement of the level of corporate globalization (LoCG) as a marketing problem

The level of corporate globalization (LoCG) is an important variable, having an impact on global customer relationships as well as on the entire performance of a firm. An overview of this underlying hypothesis is given in Figure 1.1. The major purpose of this work is to derive

Figure 1.1   Overview of the research issue

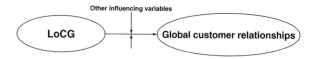

implications for global customer management (GCM), as the measurement scale can be used by managers as a tool to segment their customers and design GCM programmes according to the characteristics of customer groups belonging to different LoCGs.

In addition to this major purpose, a second interesting research question comes to mind. Researchers have already dealt with the construct of globalization and have developed several approaches focusing on the main characteristics of different levels of corporate globalization. Probably one of the most widely discussed approaches is that of Bartlett (1986; cf. also Bartlett and Ghoshal 1989; Ghoshal and Bartlett, 1998; discussed in Chapter 2 of this work), differentiating between international, multinational, global and transnational companies. It has not yet been proven empirically that these four categories really characterize companies in practice and that transnational companies exist. The research design of the present work aims to develop a measurement scale for corporate globalization to enable the empirical testing of Bartlett's categories. This testing is considered as the second research objective.

As already described, the main focus is on GCM. Therefore, a detailed problem description of this area follows. Global customer management is a strategic concept in the parent discipline of customer relationship management, used to retain customers that globalize or already act globally. However, the implementation of this concept is costly and should therefore only be offered to really global customers that demand it – with different programme strategies according to the customer's LoCG. Ideally, needs of customers and suppliers should be matched. In the GCM literature, global customers are characterized as customers that show some form of global procurement coordination, because otherwise the alleged 'global' relationship often ends up only in global pricing arrangements (cf. Hennessey, 2001, pp. 234f.).[1] Hereby, value is not created equally on both sides (that is, in the case above, the customer would not intend to purchase globally, but would only try to 'dictate' the same price worldwide) and the relationship partners cannot perpetuate a long-term relationship. The two essential questions that have to be answered now are (a) whether global procurement coordination is the only relevant characteristic of GCM for a global company (cf. GCM purpose), or (b) if there are other characteristics as well (cf. for example Bartlett's approach, that is purpose 2) and how the characteristics can be operationalized and measured. Therefore, the literature must be examined regarding clear definitions and characteristics of this construct.

The assumption of value creation on both sides is based on the principle of relationship marketing.[2] The primary goal, when thinking in customer relationships, is customer retention, because it is believed that customer retention directly pays off on the cost as well as on the revenue side (cf. Bruhn, 2001, p. 3) through positive distribution and price effects.[3] Indirect pay-off is given through mouth-to-mouth communication between customers, which can help to avoid customer migration and to acquire new customers without a company's efforts. These effects can only be realized if the company orientates itself on entire, interrelated customer relationships instead of single transactions. This implies a long-term revenue maximization and long-term fulfilment of customer needs. Then both relationship sides gain value and no opportunistic behaviour should arise.

The match of suppliers' and customers' needs requires effective customer segmentation which can be carried out by using quantitative and qualitative selection criteria (for example turnover, customer value and so on), and one of these criteria is the degree of corporate globalization. Wilson *et al.* (2002), for example, name the selection criterion 'global spread', designating if a company is global and how global it is. The degree of corporate globalization as one important factor for global customer management is often suggested in the literature (cf. Millman, 1999, pp. 3f.; Montgomery and Yip, 2000; Wilson *et al.*, 2001, p. 12), and the positive relationship between 'use of global customer management', 'demand of global customer management from customers' and 'extent of globalization' has already been proven by Montgomery and Yip (1999). It is supposed that the customers' degree of corporate globalization is essential for the success and effectiveness of a GCM programme. For this reason, the LoCG should be calculated first to determine which customers, if any, are operating globally. Only then should a second selection process

Figure 1.2   Problem definition

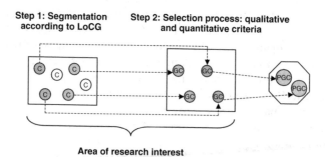

Step 1: Segmentation according to LoCG

Step 2: Selection process: qualitative and quantitative criteria

Area of research interest

C = Customer; GC = Global customer; PGC = Profitable global customer

'round' be undertaken where other qualitative and quantitative criteria are used to select the most profitable and promising customers from the global ones (cf. Figure 1.2).

Justification

Few authors have worked out the properties and dimensions of the corporate level of globalization from a marketing perspective – whereas a vast variety of literature is found in the strategic and international management area (cf. Chapter 2) – and the connection to global customer management. The importance of adequate key account selection is recognized, but few workable instructions are given. The relationship of the LoCG to global customer management is supported by the literature: the extent of corporate globalization is (1) an important selection criterion for global accounts, and (2) relates positively to the demand for GCM from customers and the use of GCM within companies.

However, the construct of LoCG has not yet been conceptualized properly – this conceptualization is the theoretical contribution of this research – nor has it been measured adequately. The attempt to measure this degree has a long tradition since Vernon's multi-national enterprise project in the 1960s. However, most approaches since then have been targeted on the degree of *internationalization* and are limited to geography-based, simple measurements (see the discussion of measurement approaches in Chapter 2) – such as the ratio of foreign employees to total employees in a company (cf. van den Berghe,

2001), the ratio of foreign assets to total assets (cf. Sullivan, 1994) and the proportion of overseas subsidiaries to total subsidiaries (cf. Ietto-Gillies, 1998; Sullivan 1994). Other approaches use indices such as the 'network-spread index' (that is, measuring the number of foreign countries in which the company has foreign subsidiaries divided by the number of countries in which the company potentially could have subsidiaries; cf. UNCTAD, 1998), or the 'transnational activities spread index' (cf. Ietto-Gillies, 1998), but the disadvantages of indices are well known. Moreover, most existing approaches focus on the industry and not on the company level, which is definitely not adequate for the research issue of this work. Very few studies have integrated multiple indicators or used multiple dimensions, and most resarchers have attempted to build theories, not measurements. Therefore, the development of a new measurement approach is necessary – and that is the methodological contribution of this work.

In the author's opinion, the subject 'globalization' requires a multi-dimensional approach to capture its complexity, because corporate globalization cannot be represented by using only simple geography-based measurements. Corporate globalization is assumed to have an impact on corporate orientation, process and strategies, and therefore the scale must include items describing attitudes, strategies, systems and structures. Purchasing decisions, important for the use of GCM programmes, are made in each value-chain activity, which implies that not all value-chain activities are globalized at once. The assumption is then that companies featuring different degrees of globalization will show different structures of globalized value-chain activities. No measurement approach could be found that takes this into account so far, but it is considered in this work. Furthermore, a measurement approach not tied to geography but to strategy integration and process coordination could also not be found, although theory-building is often undertaken exactly in that direction.

The development of a new measurement scale is essential from the managerial point of view:

1 To enable companies to use the LoCG as a segmentation criterion for their GCM target group: customers can be grouped according to their parameter values on the scale's factors. Only the 'global' customers should be included for a GCM programme because they are assumed to be the only group that purchases worldwide and demands global services;

2   To enable companies to design their GCM programmes according to their customers' needs, which are to a certain degree affected by their LoCG. The aim of this research is *not* to *adapt* the strategies, but to show which factors determine global companies because these build the basis for the design of GCM strategies;

3   To enable the determination of a company's own strategic position for deriving general strategic implications for corporate planning;

as well as from the theoretical point of view:

4   To contribute to the clarification of the dimensions of the LoCG construct and to test Bartlett's approach to transnational companies;

5   To extend the existing measurement approaches and present a multi-dimensional approach corresponding with the complexity of the construct.

Research structure

The study is structured into a theoretical part (Chapter 2) consisting of two main overall conceptual areas; namely, corporate globalization and customer-relationship management. This part includes a debate about the characteristics and indicators of globalization and the context of global customer management within the area of customer-relationship management. A description of the research methodology then follows in Chapter 3. Chapter 4 reports the results of an empirical study, divided into qualitative and quantitative sections. The qualitative study develops the items measuring globalization, and the key variables are then operationalized and transformed into a measurement scale. The quantitative part tests the item battery by means of a questionnaire sent to a sample of companies in Germany and Austria.

Finally, Chapter 5 includes theoretical and managerial implications in the context of GCM. Fields of application, limitations and future research questions are presented.

Definition of concepts

It is necessary to delimit the construct of corporate globalization from the globalization of economies, markets and other spheres (such as culture, for example), because the characteristics and dimensions that have to be taken into consideration vary depending on the point of view the researcher takes. The objective of this introductory chapter is to develop the key characteristics of *corporate* globalization. To this end, different research areas were analysed – economic, sociological, political science, business and marketing research – from a functional, attitudinal, structural and strategic angle.

We first look at the general etymological meaning of globalization. What is corporate globalization really about? An etymological consideration indicates that the meaning of 'global' stems from the Latin *globus*, which is translated as globe/world/terra. Globalization, then, interpreted as process, means to 'orientate worldwide'. To sociologists the term denotes the existence of global, open systems (cf. Beck, 1997) or the increase of worldwide social relationships which connect remote locations. Incidents in one location are influenced by operations in others (cf. Giddens, 1990; 1995, p. 85). When talking about globalization in general, one has to bear in mind the existence of different levels on which the globalization phenomenon can be observed: the globalization of economies, markets, companies and other spheres (marketing, culture and so on; see Figure 1.3).

The globalization of economies is linked to the globalization of markets. Therefore, markets are analysed economically: goods and service markets, labour markets and financial/capital markets usually develop from national markets to cross-national (=international) markets, to regional and then to global markets (see for example Heenan and Perlmutter, 1979; Kutschker and Schmid, 2002, pp. 151f.). For several

Figure 1.3   Overview of concepts

years, one has been able to observe an accelerating globalization of these markets. Capital markets are the most globalized; goods and service markets are partly globalized, but also show a great extent of regionalization; labour markets are still mostly national, and only in special segments is a trend towards globalization visible.

The globalization of companies is linked with the globalization of markets. Nunnenkamp *et al.* (1994, p. 8) argue that, 'globalization is expected to result from the perpetual search of TNCs[4] for cost efficient production sites and lucrative markets'. One strategy to globalize lies in the use of foreign direct investment (FDI),[5] another in the use of non-equity forms of international cooperation (NEC).[6] Nunnenkamp *et al.* (1994) stated a relationship between FDI and NEC such that a rise in FDI causes less globalization through NEC. However, both FDI and NEC in general have a high growth potential.

The level of corporate globalization represents the focus of this research. However, it is also dependent on the kind of *industry*. Many authors suggest that companies within a specific industry are exposed to the same conditions, and therefore tend to use the same business model to pursue competition (see for example Morrison, 1990). But according to today's perception, different business models exist in parallel, which implies that different companies within one industry can have a varying degree of globalization and therefore use different strategies (see for example Kutschker and Schmid, 2002, p. 155). This is the reason why research is undertaken at company and not at industry level, although most authors, especially in the corporate strategy area, concentrate on the industry level (see for example Hamel and Prahalad; Lorange, Morton and Ghoshal, 1986; Porter, 1986a,b, 1993).

The globalization of other spheres includes the globalization of culture, politics, law ethics, ecology, and science as well as technology, communication and media. The development of communication and information technologies is the fundamental basis for globalization in general, and also especially for enabling corporate globalization (see for example Nunnenkamp *et al.*, 1994, p. 2; or Parker, 1998, pp. 73ff.). These technologies highlight the borders and the rising interdependency between nations, societies and companies: the world is shrinking as a consequence of the emerging coalescence ('global village'). This phenomenon of convergence can be observed in many research areas: economics, business, sociology, political science or marketing, to name only a few.

Sociologists, for example, state that the convergence of culture is already visible in terms of a certain degree of uniformity; anglicization of languages, similar foods and fashions worldwide and similar business practices (see Fraedrich, Herndon and Ferrell, 1995; Parker, 1998; Swimme, 1984; Tomlinson, 1991; Tully, 1994). This is especially observable within the young generation. Ohmae (1990) calls it a 'borderless world', and Reich (1991) the 'end of the nation state'. The literature in marketing and international management often refers to the expression 'universal customer needs' to denote the phenomenon that people, irrespective of home country, want the same products.

Economists have developed concepts to explain globalization, for example through factor-price theories (for example Kleinert *et al.*, 2000). Economic geographers have stated that a global world consists of many regions integrated through production chains (for example Scott, 1998; Storper, 1997). Also the 'country-of-origin question' ('Does nationality matter?') is still of importance as firms originating from small countries have a higher propensity to internationalize. Moreover, political decisions within a country must be taken in the light of international politics: laws and taxes must be adapted. The consequences of increased globalization are the erosion of state power and sovereignty and the narrowing of national government policy margins (cf. for example Stopford *et al.*, 1991; van den Berghe, 2001).

The business point of view is taken into account because it focuses especially on the corporate level and because the complexity of strategic decision-making increases. Corporate globalization can be 'interpreted as an entrepreneurial response to a changing environment, while the leitmotiv of firm behaviour – constrained profit maximisation – remains unchanged' (Nunnenkamp *et al.*, 1994, p. 2). In the business field, the globalization process has enabled competition almost free of national interventions, which in turn brings to light the advantages and disadvantages of locational conditions. The rivalry between locations set on a global level provides an opportunity for companies to produce low-priced goods, and leads to more customer orientation. Globalization means more operational and optional opportunities for companies and consumers, but national differentiation – and therefore individualization – is an important area in many industries, too. This is the reason for the oft cited advice that a globalized company should 'think global but act local'.

Corporate globalization is also an important issue in the field of marketing. As markets globalize, great demands are made on marketing departments including decisions on market entry strategies (cf. for example the OLI-paradigma of Dunning, 1988, Kotabe and Helsen, 2001 or Wührer, 1995), adapted marketing strategies and cultural-influence issues. However, corporate globalization not only plays a major role in the classical transaction marketing approach, but also in the relationship marketing approach. This can be explained in two ways by looking at both the customer–vendor relationship as well as the supplier–producer relationship. On the one hand it is explained by the nature of customer–vendor relationships (B2C – business to consumer), which build on the constructs trust, commitment and loyalty, with cultural influences and differences having an important impact. Relationship strategies must take this into consideration. On the other hand, the importance of globalization in the relationship-marketing approach can be explained by the supplier–producer relationship (B2B – business-to-business). If one party globalizes, it simultaneously expects the other party to offer globalized services and products, a single price worldwide, as well as a single point of contact. A match between both parties is necessary to obtain satisfaction and success on both sides. At this level of globalization, the standardization principle is widely used to unitize the sales approach across the entire company.

*   *   *

To develop key characteristics by which corporate globalization can be measured, it is necessary to examine the literature on globalization and the globalized firm to demarcate it from the terms internationalization and the internationalized company and multinational enterprize (MNE): virtually no single definition of what 'global' really means exists; what one author defines as global is called transnational by the next (cf. specifications in Chapter 2). Moreover, different opinions exist regarding the umbrella term: is it internationalization, where globalization is defined as a special form of internationalization, or is it globalization where the international approach is a stage in the process of globalization. And is it a process or is it a matter of separate categorization? Globalization can be defined as a process when the term is used as a generic term for strategies to orientate worldwide. But globalization can also be defined as a discrete variable, when the term is used for categorizing different strategies to internationalize: international, multinational and global strategies. This leads to a separation of different degrees or levels of globalization. Beamish *et al.* (2000) argue that it is international strategy which has two possible parameter values: multidomestic or global. Other authors such as Heenan and Perlmutter (1979) or Ghoshal and Bartlett (1998) categorize different types of approaches to gain foreign markets and draw distinct borders. The term globalization is thus used loosely and is often equated with internationalization. What is of great importance is the question of process and categorization, and in this work we adopt the categorization approach (see for example Ghoshal and Bartlett, 1998; Heenan and Perlmutter, 1979; Parvatiyar and Gruen, 2001). Categorization is necessary to be able to draw borders between different LoCGs, otherwise no measurement would be possible, and in the following chapter all terms used in the literature will be structured and compared.

From a marketing point of view, the issue of globalization is mostly addressed in the field of global marketing and key account management. Here, a variety of literature can be found, and that on global account management is especially relevant for the research questions underlying this work. Again, this will be discussed in the following chapter.

Two key issues can be found: the principles of coordination and integration. Wilson (1999, p. 31) defines a global customer as a 'multinational customer that has a coordinated procurement and decision making process', whereas an international customer is described as an 'account with locations in different parts of the world, but with a decentralised decision making process' (Wilson, 1999, p. 31). But this represents an orientation which most authors commonly would call multinational/multidomestic or polycentric.

Montgomery and Yip (2000) define a new challenge for multinational suppliers to multinational customers dealing on a global basis, which encompasses global contracts, service quality, prices and products. To meet this demand, suppliers must centralize and integrate globally. Global account management[7] can enhance customer satisfaction, revenues and profits, but a precondition for success is the stage of corporate globalization of both the customer and the supplier. Only if the customer demands worldwide integrated purchasing, service and so on, and the supplier can respond accordingly (that is, adopt a global strategy), can a GCM programme be implemented successfully.

Montgomery and Yip provide a framework for GCM that involves the identification of an industry's globalization drivers (for both customer and supplier, for example global sourcing), the demand for GCM by customers as well as the readiness of suppliers to supply such services (both depend on the organizational heritage and *stage of globalization*), and the consideration of the performance effect. The drivers as well as organization heritage affect a customer's potential as a global account. Montgomery and Yip (2000, p. 4) measure this potential by the 'percentage of the [customers'] purchases made on a globally coordinated basis'. For the supplier, the measure is, vice versa, the 'percentage of revenues accounted for by customers buying on a globally centralized basis'. They also found in their study that revenues stemming from really globally coordinated customers make up about 13 per cent of the total, whereas from all international customers it makes up about 46 per cent and from multinational ones 26 per cent. According to these numbers one could hypothesize that the beginning of foreign activity is at an international level, followed by a development towards the multinational level and then towards the global level. This hypothesis can be tested by asking questionnaire respondents when they started foreign activity and linking this variable to their measured levels of corporate globalization. However, this statement also makes clear that a theoretical differentiation between 'international', 'global' and 'multinational' cannot be drawn meaningfully as all these terms have already been flogged to death. Instead, it seems to be more precise to classify the companies empirically according to the factors and items that are intended to characterize the different forms of international companies and to interpret the resulting clusters regarding the theoretically suggested terms 'global', 'international' and 'multinational'.

One can of course criticize the chosen title 'levels of corporate globalization' as the construct 'global' cannot be clearly separated from the other theoretical constructs 'international' or 'transnational'. To focus on the main GCM problem behind this discussion, namely world-wide coordinated procurement decisions as the relevant criterion for choosing GCM strategies for customers, one could choose, for example, the 'degree of coordination of procurement' as the construct title. However, the aim of this research is not only a segmentation approach for GCM, but also the testing whether the theoretically intended forms or degrees of foreign activities (cf. the national integration–national differentiation grid of Bartlett, 1986; see below pp. 24 ff.) correspond to practice. Therefore, 'globalization' is maintained as the umbrella term for all different degrees of foreign activity or procurement coordination, although the definitional difficulties and varieties in theory are well known.

The question is, which dimensions characterize this construct of corporate globalization? Companies having a high LoCG are expected to show a distinctive occurrence of interdependence, integration and coordination of value-chain activities (that is, of strategies, programmes and processes) as well as certain, if any, occurrences of centralization and standardization. National differentiation is seen as typical for rarely coordinated (that is multinational) companies, but it can be of importance when considering a complex global (that is, transnational) company which loads not only on integration and interdependence, but at the same time on national differentiation. Geography is used to characterize internationally operating companies which also show a certain degree of centralization and standardization and less coordination.

As it is difficult to draw borders between different degrees of corporate globalization by definition, the classification of the investigated companies will be performed inductively as already mentioned. One hypothesis is that only a very small portion of fully coordinated (that is, fully globalized) companies (transnational companies in Bartlett's words) exist (cf. the empirical test of Bartlett and Ghoshal's organizational typology by Leong and Tan, 1993). But for implications regarding GCM, the area of 'simple' global enterprises that are globally integrated but have a low level of local differentiation and only a certain degree of coordination is also of interest. But local differentiation and global integration are only two constituting dimensions, and in the author's opinion the subject requires a multi-dimensional approach. As the aim is to cluster companies according to their degree of corporate globalization in the different categories (the empirical classification brings up the categories), all factors characterizing these categories have to be considered. These were already named above and are the dimensions integration, interdependence, national differentiation/decentralization, centralization and standardization. In addition, the value-chain activities are included to test the hypothesis that different activities are carried out locally or coordinated globally according to the level of corporate globalization.

The relevant literature for this research objective is in the strategic and international management and marketing area, and I shall therefore concentrate on both the management (that is, the corporate globalization issues and characteristics) and the marketing (that is, the global customer-relationship management issues) perspectives (see Chapter 2).

of globalization'. The studies and approaches summarized in Table 2.4 are discussed in detail below.

The first field described in detail (business viewpoint) is the research area of global strategy. Authors who have worked on global strategic concepts include Bartlett (1986), Bartlett and Ghoshal (1987; 1988), Ghoshal (1993), Heenan and Perlmutter (1979), Hout, Porter and Rudden (1982) and Kogut (1985). Some of the authors and theories will be explained here, but one has to note that most strategic concepts focus on drivers and characteristics of globalization at the industry level and seldom at the corporate level.

Perlmutter (1969) is counted among the pioneers in international business and developed the well-known EPRG scheme to represent a firm's world view as a basis for its decisions on global strategy. E stands for ethnocentric, P for polycentric, R for regiocentric and G for geocentric. This scheme describes the types of headquarters orientation (which builds on attitudes of companies) towards subsidiaries in an MNC (see for example Heenan and Perlmutter, 1979, p. 17ff.) and is based on the attitudinal level of a company. An ethnocentric view implies that home country employees are given key positions in subsidiaries throughout the world in the belief that they are more capable of handling business there. The geographical identification is identical with the nationality of the owner. Polycentric oriented companies allow subsidiaries to carry out their own business because of the assumption that cultures of different countries are dissimilar and therefore difficult to understand and manage from the home base. As long as the profit-making criterion is met, nobody from headquarters cares about coordination or control. The geographical identification here is therefore the host country's nationality. In the author's opinion, the polycentric orientation circumscribes what is defined as a multinational company. A regiocentric orientation implies the establishment of human resources on a regional basis; that is, people are recruited and trained in the respective region. The firm identifies itself as a regional company with high authority in a single regional headquarters with collaboration between subsidiaries. The geocentric view tries to 'integrate diverse regions through a global systems approach to decision making' (Heenan and Perlmutter, 1979, p. 20). Here, headquarters and subsidiaries identify themselves as parts of a worldwide entity. An MNC is described as competent when it optimally allocates resources on a global basis. Moreover, it is evaluated on universal and local standards and employs international and local employees at the same location. This view defines integration as the key principle.

To achieve a balance between global integration and national adaptation, one must consider the important role of coordination mechanisms as facilitating instruments. The literature supports and examines this role: Martinez and Jarillo (1991), for example, conducted a study of 50 subsidiaries of MNCs to examine the relationship 'between the strategy of an MNC – defined as its choice of integration and differentiation levels across its geographically dispersed organization units – and the mechanisms of coordination used to implement that strategy' (1991, p. 430). The hypothesis tested and confirmed was that a high degree of integration between subsidiary and corporate parent implies a high use of mechanisms of coordination. Coordination of manufacturing activities with R&D, engineering and marketing on a global basis is the core of an integrated global strategy, and the principle of integration is seen as a key requirement of the globalization of industries (cf. Kutschker and Schmid, 2002). This point of view is also supported by Beamish *et al.* (2000), Doz (1986), Leontiades (1985), Porter (1986a,b) and Prahalad and Doz (1987). The importance of integration and coordination as principles of globalization is also stated in the global acount management literature (for example Wilson, Speare and Reese, 2002), as described at the beginning of this work, and is not limited to international business approaches. Therefore, literature in this field supports the author's view that coordination is an important dimension of the construct 'global', and that it probably increases the higher a company's LoCG, because it can be explained that companies working all over the world have to deal with complex decisions (on strategies, programmes, processes and operational activities such as purchasing, for example) and situations that can only be handled through close coordination and worldwide integration.

In the GCM area, the coordination dimension is especially relevant when companies decide to purchase globally from a supplier. Therefore, this value-chain activity is probably one of the first activities to be globalized and it is assumed that not all value-chain activities must be globalized at the same time or show the same LoCG. Porter (1986) is one researcher who attended to the level of value-chain activities, discussing the configuration of a firm's value chain to obtain the best possible advantages from global integration and national differentiation. Leontiades (1984) also described a firm's structure of the flow of tasks as the basis for an explanation of global strategy, stating that the more integrated and rationalized the flow of tasks, the more global the strategy. According to these considerations, the hypothesis is presented that a typical order exists in which the value-chain activities are globalized.

The second dimension we wish to study is the responsiveness to local markets; that is, differentiation (see also Bartlett, 1986; Doz, 1986; Hamel and Prahalad, 1985; and Porter, 1986a,b), sometimes also called localization. Hamel and Prahalad (1985) view a broad product/service portfolio as well as many product varieties – that is, an implicit assumption of differentiation – as the key point. In addition, they consider cross-subsidization across products and markets as well as global resource allocation as another essential part of a global strategy.

It is therefore assumed that both global integration and local differentiation are demanded simultaneously in the globalizing world; but this can only be achieved by internal coordination (cf. Bartlett and Ghoshal, 1990; Martinez and Jarillo, 1991, p. 429f.). Martinez and Jarillo (1989) analysed a variety of different studies on coordination mechanisms and found a trend in the studies conducted recently towards analysing mostly subtle coordination mechanisms. This may be due to the fact that MNCs' managers use more and more subtle and informal coordination mechanisms as a consequence of changes in the environment. Thus, environmental changes influence the type of competition at the industry level, which in turn leads to a strategic adaptation, modifying organizational and structural patterns, and is reflected – among other things – by the general coordination mechanisms (cf. Martinez and Jarillo, 1989, p. 500). It could also be, of course, that researchers have become more sophisticated and therefore better understand those subtle mechanisms. Yet, the first explanation seems of significant relevance, which is also confirmed by Bartlett and Ghoshal (1987) who stated that the need for simultaneous responsiveness to different strategic demands underlines a sophisticated set of coordination mechanisms, namely informal/subtle ones. Only under this condition does a company have enough flexibility to respond to local differences and at the same time use global opportunities.

The use of coordination mechanisms, whether formal or informal, can build a basis for realizing global integration and local differentiation, and therefore such mechanisms belong to the main constituting elements of corporate globalization. The mix of integrative devices is therefore taken as one possible variable for the measurement scale. Realizing global integration and local differentiation simultaneously needs subtle coordination mechanisms and, therefore, leads to the hypothesis that a company's coordination issues in the sense of normative integration (cf. Perlmutter's EPRG scheme with the development from a polycentric to a geocentric orientation and coordination by use of culture, values and so on) increase during the development of its operations from national to global. Moreover, the rise in interdependence leads to a rise in integration of subsidiaries and their corporate parents. This is also confirmed by Hout *et al.* (1982) who advance interdependence (interpreted as interdependent management for achieving synergies across a company's activities) and investments (for obtaining preemptive positions) as principles of a successful global strategy (besides the exploitation of economies of scale reached only by offering a global volume of products/services).

Product standardization is often stated to be the key to a global strategy (cf. Levitt, 1983) in the literature. However, this does not correspond to the arguments given above and the discussion in the previous chapter. The present author agrees with Levitt in the sense that standardization plays a role within a gobal company, but to a lesser degree than suggested by Levitt, and standardization must not be limited to the product level. Products, for example, are standardized in global companies as far as possible, but are *localized wherever needed* (cf., for example, the results of the expert interviews presented in Chapter 4). Also, processes or systems can be standardized to facilitate global integration, an aspect not considered by Levitt.

In this author's opinion, standardization is the key characteristic of an international strategy. Levitt does not clearly delimit the terms global and international (see also Zupancic and Senn, 2000). Our focus is different: within international companies, headquarters mostly define strategies and delegate them, that is, act in a centralized way. This principle of centralization is consistent with the viewpoint of Bartlett and Ghoshal (1989), Ghoshal and Bartlett (1998) who speak of the *central ized* hub company. Standardization simplifies the process of acting in this centralized way. Therefore, centralization and standardization accurately describe the international company. Levitt's definition is reflected in Porter's types of international strategy (cf. Figure 2.2) in the field called 'purest global strategy' a field characterized by a high degree of coordination and geographical concentration. The difference between this interpretation and the author's delimitation given in the previous chapter lies in the fact that Porter and Levitt mark international strategy as an umbrella term for all categories (inclusive 'global') whilst this work interprets international and global as two distinct categories constituting two different levels of corporate globalization. Being global means integrating diverse regions through, for example, a global systems approach to decision making (cf. the 'geocentric view' of Heenan and Perlmutter, 1979).

Turning to our second research objective, Bartlett and Ghoshal (1989) and Ghoshal and Bartlett (1998) developed a framework consisting of four different structural options: decentralized federation, coordinated federation, centralized hub and transnational federation. It is our intention to test this framework. The decentralized federation is characterized by local identification and exploitation of opportunities and local self-sufficiency in resourcing – also known as the multinational strategy. The coordinated federation adapts core competencies of the parent corporation and sources centrally – the global strategy. The centralized hub is defined by centralization and implementation of corporate strategies – described as the international option. The transnational strategy enhances diverse but interdependent perspectives as well as capability exploitation, supported by flexible coordination and a shared corporate vision (Figure 2.1).

Figure 2.1 National integration–differentiation grid

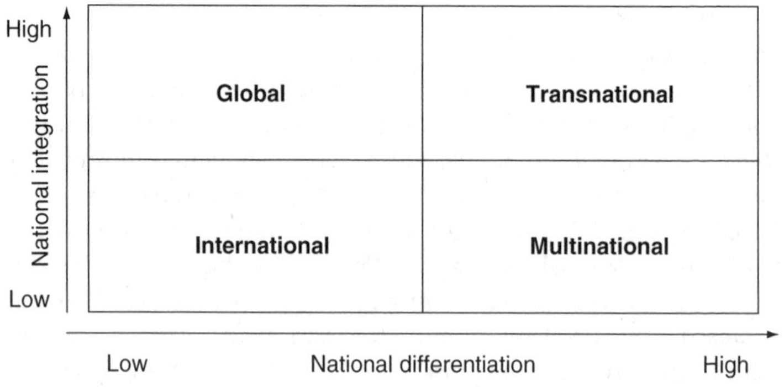

Source: Based on Bartlett, 1986, in Porter (1986b); p. 377.

The characteristics of a transnational company lie in:

1 *Multinational perspectives*: a strong national subsidiary management, capable global business management and influential functional management are the main factors constituting transnational companies;
2 *Distribution of capabilities, resources, knowledge, etc.*: each subsidiary should concentrate on what it does best, to enable the building of a network structure that in turn increases the worldwide interdependence of units. The consequence is an integrated network of distributed and interrelated resources and capabilities. This distribution can be pursued on three different levels: transfer of assets and resources to the country level, transfer of knowledge and skills for effective use, and transfer of tasks and responsibilities to allow locals to develop their potential and contribute to the network (cf. Bartlett, in Porter, 1986b, pp. 381f.);
3 *Flexible integrative management processes*: to differentiate relationships and decision-making roles by function, across businesses, among geographic units and over time. This differentiation can be supported through the management of the organizational context, to include the establishment and communication of clear objectives, development of managing individuals with worldwide perspectives and open mindsets, as well as the promotion of norms and rules (for example, through formal and informal reward systems for keeping the rules). Moreover, the management of organizational processes (that is, structure roles and relationships in key decisions) as well as the management of the content of issues (that is, open handling of conflicts) encourage the integrative management process.

Regarding the characteristics of the construct 'global', Bartlett and Ghoshal's approach summarizes what has been discussed so far and does not add new characteristics. However, this approach is the first that builds a classification system for companies that show different characteristics and that, therefore, belong to different LoCG groups. Our second research objective is the empirical testing as to whether this classification exists in practice.

Porter (1993, p. 147) gives an overview of configuration and coordination issues on the value-chain activity level (summarized in Table 2.1).

Table 2.1 Configuration and coordination issues by category of activity

Value activities	Configuration issues	Coordination issues (worldwide)
Operations	Location of production facilities	Networking; transferring process technology and production know-how
Marketing and sales	Product-line selection; country (market) selection	Commonality of brand name; coordination of sales; similarity of channels and product positioning; coordination of pricing
Service	Location of service organization	Similarity of service standards
Technology development	Number and location of R&D centres	Interchange among dispersed R&D centres; products responsive to market needs in many countries
Procurement	Location of the purchasing function	Managing suppliers located in different countries; transferring market knowledge

Source: Based on Porter, in Lecraw, Morrison and Dunning (1993), p. 147, with the permission of Routledge.

'Configuration' indicates where in the world as well as in how many places the value-chain activities are performed. The accomplishing of activities ranges on a continuum from concentrated to dispersed. 'Coordination' indicates the issues necessary to master the value-chain activities across different countries.

This overview offers useful categories for the empirical part of our work, since Porter has already interrelated issues such as configuration and coordination with value-chain activities, within his dimensions of international strategy. In addition, he identified different types of international strategy, and a summary based on his approach is shown in Figure 2.2.

The four strategies described in the fields of Figure 2.2 show some similarities and differences with Bartlett and Ghoshal's approach. Similarities are especially found in the coordination dimension. The top-left quadrant represents Bartlett and Ghoshal's transnational company, whilst the quadrant beneath characterizes to a large extent the

Figure 2.2 Types of international strategy

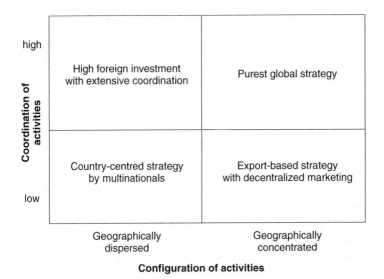

Source: Based on Porter, in Lecraw, Morrison and Dunning (1993), p. 149, with the permission of Routledge.

'decentralized federation', alias Bartlett and Ghoshal's multinational company. Porter's approach fits well in providing hints for our scale development because of the additional functional level of consideration (that is, referring to the single value-chain activites, equated with a company's functional levels). This author's suggestion is to combine the approaches of Porter and of Bartlett and Ghoshal into an integrated whole. Therefore, selected items from Porter, especially the third dimension of the value-chain activities, will be included in the questionnaire for our quantitative analysis (for example, interchange among dispersed R&D centres is included, as well as the similarity of service standards and procedures worldwide or the transfer of process technology and production know-how among plants). The dimensions of coordination/integration as well as national differentiation are taken from Bartlett and Ghoshal. A detailed description of the items used in the survey is given later in the chapter. The items are based on the suggestions found in literature and empirical studies, as well as on the qualitative part of our analysis (the specifications are given in Chapter 4).

In addition, the framework for defining various global strategies developed by Hamel and Prahalad (1993) is included, which is built on the dimensions of competitive advantage (location, world-scale volume and global brand distribution) and strategic intent (building global presence, defending a domestic position and overcoming national fragmentation). Moreover, Hamel and Prahalad distinguish between global competition, global business and the global company. Global companies are characterized by having 'distribution systems in key foreign markets that enable cross-subsidization, international retaliation, and world-scale volume'[8] (1993, pp. 125ff.). This approach also supports the hypothesis that not all value-chain activities must be globalized at once, because it assumes that distribution must be globalized to speak of a 'global' company.

Kogut (1985) also follows this approach: his characteristics are multiple sourcing, production shifting (to benefit from varying factor costs and exchange rates) and arbitrage (which he defines as the opportunity to exploit financial and informational market imperfections).

Ghoshal (1987) examined and compared all these different approaches and drew the conclusion that no organizing framework, designed to help compare and assimilate all the different theories, exists. In developing a framework, Ghoshal faced the problems of the subject's multidimensionality and the difficulty of prioritizing particular dimensions. He considered that distinguishing between global and multidomestic strategies does not help managers decide on strategic issues. According to him, a better framework might use key strategic objectives of MNCs and the tools for achieving them (Table 2.2).

Achieving efficiency in current operations is defined as maximizing efficiency rents, if the different resources are available. The risks can be separated into macroeconomic, political (from policy actions of governments), competitive and resource risks (cf. Ghoshal, 1993, pp. 177f.). The last strategic objective named by Ghoshal is based on the assumption that diversity of environments offers stimuli/potential for learning. Of course, respective mechanisms that enable learning to take place are needed. The sources of competitive advantage reflect (according to the author of this work) the principles differentiation (= national differences) and standardization (= scale economies). Economies of scope can be reached, for example, by increased integration of related

Table 2.2 Global strategy: an organizing framework

Strategic objectives	Sources of competitive advantage		
	National differences	*Scale economies*	*Scope economies*[9]
Achieving efficiency	Benefiting from differences in factor costs	Expanding and exploiting potential scale economies	Sharing of investments and costs
Managing risks	Managing different kinds of risks	Balancing scale with flexibility	Portfolio diversification of risks
Innovation learning and adaptation	Learning from societal differences	Benefiting from experience	Shared learning across organization

Source: Based on Ghoshal, 1987, in Lecraw, Morrison and Dunning (eds) (1993), p. 174, with the permission of Routledge.

activities. Standardization is one thesis defined by Levitt, already mentioned, which was refused because of its strong concentration on internationalization,[10] not on globalization. The other principle – differentiation is often confronted with Levitt's thesis. Regarding the trend to flexible automation (for example, mass customization), this thesis seems more appropriate. However, differentiation alone is not enough as it would characterize multinational enterprises. Global enterprises, on the other hand, are in the author's opinion advanced from multinationals. Therefore, Table 2.2 is only partly considered as helpful in developing measurement scales.

In this theoretical framework the main characteristics of corporate globalization have been discussed and the research hypotheses derived from this discussion. A summary of the hypotheses is given later in the chapter ('Research issues', pp. 59ff.). The discussion has clearly shown that not all considerations of corporate globalization in the literature fit the author's comprehension and research purpose. To conclude, the main approach the author adopts in this research is that of Bartlett (1986) Bartlett and Ghoshal (1989) and Ghoshal and Bartlett (1998), because (1) this approach summarizes all characteristics discussed individually by other authors and builds a basic framework; and (2) the classification of companies according to different LoCGs is also the purpose of this research and enables an empirical examination of the theoretically assumed classification structure. The considerations of other authors regarding single dimensions and characteristics have either been taken as supports for our argument, or deemed inappropriate for this research. The key dimensions (characteristics) from the different studies according to the author's own systematization will be summarized later in the chapter.

Measurement approaches

The field of international business has a long tradition in trying to measure the degree of internationalization, but hardly any study could be found that deals explicitly with the measurement of the degree of corporate globalization. The question arises why this is the case. First of all, although many attempts have been made, little progress is visible and the measurement attempts were often based on data availability rather than on conceptual reasoning (cf. van den Berghe, 2001, p. 6; original discussion in Ramaswamy, Kroeck and Renforth, 1996). Moreover, many international measurement approaches can be found but only few global ones.

Van den Berghe (2001) tried to conceptualize the construct of corporate internationalization which, according to him, relates to the 'level of foreign involvement of [an] MNE in one or more host economies... and the primary goal...should be to measure the increase or decrease in foreign involvement as opposed to domestic involvement' (2001, p. 6f.). Van den Berghe also discusses the problem of internationalization with and without firm growth, that is, in cases where internationalization goes together with expansion. According to him, an indicator of internationalization should address this relationship.

In what follows, the single-measurement approaches are analysed. In general, indicators of internationalization are mostly structured into structural, performance and attitudinal indicators.

One study is the measurement of the degree of internationalization (DOI) by Sullivan (1994).[11] He developed an *index* including the variables 'ratio of foreign assets to total assets' and 'proportion of overseas subsidiaries to total subsidiaries' (subsumed under the factor 'structural attribute'), 'psychic dispersion of international operations' and 'top managers' international experience' (=attitudinal attributes), as well as the 'ratio of foreign sales to total sales' (=performance attribute). However, this approach assumes the substitutability of the variables (one high score equals one low score in the result as the single scores are added up) as well as the unidimensionality of the construct DOI. The 'ratio of foreign sales to total sales' is one of the most common unidimensional single-variable indicators used, and can be found in many other scientific works (see for example Dunning and Pearce, 1981). It should be noted, however, that the content validity of the constituting elements (that is, all the variables listed above) is not tested, and this is especially important when using this particular indicator for measurements in different countries when the researcher must seek a uniform understanding of the meaning of the variables. This is especially of importance when talking about 'psychic dispersion', for example, which could be differently interpreted depending on a country's culture.

The 'ratio of foreign assets to total assets' reflects the dependence on overseas production. The 'ratio of overseas subsidiaries to total subsidiaries' is also used as a single indicator and can be found, for example, as the 'ratio of foreign affiliates to total affiliates' in Ietto-Gillies (1998). This indicator is again based on the dichotomy between foreign versus home countries. The indicator 'top managers' experience' is only conjectural, and according to Kobrin (1994) could be replaced by the quality of the experience: Kobrin examined the relationship between mindsets (the geocentric mindset is associated with a broad geographic scope of the firm) and internationalization. Finally, this research concentrates only on strategies of direct foreign investment and has no focus on customer management itself. In consequence, it provides indicators for scale development for which the methodology used is not appropriate.[12]

A unidimensional indicator is also the 'ratio of foreign employment to total employment'. This reflects the extent of a company's dependence on foreign labour markets as well as the creation of international direct employment. The employment level is often seen as a better indicator of the degree of internationalization, and can be determined easily and in a cost-efficient way. But it has to be considered that companies have often grown through mergers and acquisitions and destroy rather than create employment abroad.[13] Moreover, depending on the purpose of the measurement, it must be considered if the indirect foreign employment created by foreign subsidiaries (which emerges when MNEs outsource their activities) should be taken into consideration when calculating the indicator (cf. van den Berghe, 2001, pp. 15f.).

Another aggregated index is the Transnationality Index (UNCTAD, 1998; van den Berghe, 2001), which contains the indicators 'foreign assets to total assets', 'foreign sales to total sales' and 'foreign employment to total employment'. This index is calculated as the average of all three ratios, which are highly correlated.

The Network-Spread Index measures the number of foreign countries in which a company has foreign subsidiaries divided by the number of countries in which the company could potentially have subsidiaries. The latter number is approximately 178 based on data from the UNCTAD *World Investment Report 1998*, and is the number of countries where FDI took place in 1997 minus the home country of the firm (that is, minus 1). This index is again geography-based. It neither takes into consideration which activities are performed in the various subsidiaries and the intensity of those activities, nor other dimensions determining the level of corporate globalization (see Chapter 1, pp. 6f.).

Ietto-Gillies (1998) tried to solve this problem by integrating the Transnationality Index and the Network-Spread Index into the 'Transnational Activities Spread Index' (TASI). This index multiplies the components of the transnationality index with the network-spread index of each firm, to produce three spread indicators; namely, any 'asset spread index', 'sales spread index' and 'employment-spread index'. The average of these constitutes the TASI. The more activities exist abroad and the higher the spread of these activities in foreign countries, the higher is the degree of internationalization (Ietto-Gillies, 1998, p. 29).

The share of R&D activities abroad is another measurement possibility which was used by Cantwell (1989) and which led to the development of the Research and Development Intensity Indicator (RDI) (van den Berghe, 2001, p. 19).

Another category of measurement approaches is based upon the question of ownership; for example, the proportion of non-nationals on the board of an MNE, the proportion of shares owned by foreigners, the number of foreign stockmarkets on which the company is listed, and the use of international accounting standards.

Hassel *et al.* (2000) developed an aggregated, cross-dimensional index based on two dimensions: a real dimension of foreign activities (ratio of foreign sales to total sales, foreign employment to total employment and spread index of foreign subsidiaries) and a financial dimension (a combination of the single measures proportion of non-nationals in the board of the MNE, proportion of shares owned by foreigners, number of foreign stockmarkets on which the company is listed, and the use of international accounting standards).

In general, it has to be stated that the choice of any one of the measures described above depends heavily on the research question. According to the research question of this work, it becomes clear that the approaches described above are not adequate to measure all dimensions of globalization; almost all of them described unidimensional, single variable indices, and only a very few studies have integrated multiple indicators or used multiple dimensions. The disadvantages of aggregations are also well known. The subject 'globalization', in the author's opinion, requires a multi-dimensional approach.

The two following measurement approaches focus especially on (corporate) globalization, and correspond better to this work's research question. One approach is presented by Hu (1992): since becoming global can also be represented by becoming a stateless company, the measure of the extent of statelessness is examined. According to Hu the extent can be surveyed by the following questions:

- 'Where are the bulk of assets and people found?
- In which nation is the firm ownership located and who owns and controls foreign subsidiaries?
- What are the nationalities of senior executives at headquarters and decision makers in subsidiaries abroad?
- What is the legal nationality of the firm and to what nation does it turn for political or diplomatic protection?
- Can tax authorities in a nation choose to tax corporate earnings worldwide?' (Yao-Su Hu, 1992, p. 121)

However, this approach does not provide any empirical hints on how to use these questions for measuring corporate globalization. It seems to be more of a conceptual approach, which was not empirically tested – at least the author of this work could not find any corresponding study.

The second approach is named the A.T. Kearney Globalization Index® and focuses on globalization at the country level. This index divides the dimensions of globalization in technology and non-technology with the underlying factors and the indices: 'communication technology' (operationalized by percentage of population online, number of internet hosts per capita and number of secure servers per capita; = technology factors) as well as 'personal contact' (operationalized by data on international travel, international phone calls, cross-border remittances and other transfers), 'trade in goods and services' (measured by changing/share of international trade in each country's economy and permeability of national borders measured by convergence of domestic and international prices) and 'capital flows' (operationalized by inward and outward direct foreign investment and portfolio capital flows, income payments and receipts) which are the non-technology factors. This study is useful for getting a first impression of factors that constitute the construct, but it is not obvious how the construct has been validated and how the index has been constructed.

For measuring the customer's and the supplier's stage of globalization another framework is provided by Montgomery and Yip (2000, p. 6). However, this approach is not a measurement, but rather a classification approach and therefore cannot add to the development of our measurement scale. This classification can only be tested empirically by grouping the sample companies according to their LoCG (cf. research purpose with Bartlett's classification approach). The classification scheme is presented below:

1 *Domestic company*: most of the revenues come from the home market and domestic customers are served primarily;
2 *International company*: significant percentage of revenues comes from international activities, and products and processes are distinguished between domestic and foreign customers; a separate international division within the company can often be found;
3 *Multinational/multilocal company*: characterized by extensive international revenues and activities; the needs of local customers in local markets are served with limited coordination across borders; strong country organizations (acting more or less independently) and value-chain activities duplicated around the world are typical;

4 *Global company*: key strategic decisions are made globally integrated and the products and processes are global with opportunities for local adaptation at minimal costs; the value chain is geographically specialized and networked.

The conclusion of this analysis of existing measurement approaches is the need to develop a new measurement approach. An overview of measurement approaches examined is given in Table 2.3.

Literature review at a glance

A summarized presentation of the literature review is given in Table 2.4 along the dimensions of authors and dimensions of globalisation. For each 'dimension' is given a summary (in subject indices) of the main indicators of globalization discussed in the particular studies. The studies are differentiated according to their main dimensions in explaining/defining globalization. Six different dimensions can be identified – integration, standardization, inderdependence, differentiation, centralization and resource allocation – and for each study the indicators and concepts (structured by authors) describing the dimensions are presented.

**Key characteristics and types of corporate globalization –
a syllabus**

All the terms and classifications for the level of corporate globalization used in the literature will now be compared. Each company belonging to a certain category shows a different level of corporate globalization (that is, is a different 'type' of company). It is probable that globalization is an ongoing development process, and not every industry and company has to be at the same development level. After each type is described in detail, all dimensions and indicators found in the literature are summarized.

1 The first category of companies dealing in foreign markets is called multinational, multidomestic, multilocal or polycentric – sometimes also including the ethnocentric view as the 'very beginning' of foreign activity. Parvatiyar and Gruen (2001) call this category the 'global aspirant'. It can be characterized as a decentralized

Table 2.3 Syllabus of measurement approaches

Author(s)	Year	Research focus	Indicators of globalization (measurement)
Kobrin, S.J.	1991	Industry level	Intra-firm trade, technological intensity
Morrison, A.J. and Roth, K.	1992	Industry level	Level of international trade, intensity of international competition, worldwide product standardization (scale economies), presence of competitors in all key international markets
Sullivan, L.	1994	Corporate level	*Structural attributes* (ratio of foreign assets to total assets, the proportion of overseas subsidiaries to total subsidiaries), *attitudinal attributes* (e.g. top managers' international experience) and *performance attribute* (ratio of foreign sales to total sales)
Makhija, M.V., Kim, K., and Williamson, S.D.	1997	Industry level	Integrated global, simple global, multidomestic transitional and multidomestic: measured by level of international linkages (=extent of industry's international trade in relation to market size) and level of integration of value-added activities (=intra-industry trade)
Ietto-Gillies, G.	1998	Corporate level	*Network-spread index* (NSI): measures the ratio of foreign countries in which an MNE has foreign affiliates to the number of countries in which a firm potentially could have affiliates
			Transnational activities spread index (TASI): the higher the percentage of activities and the spread of such activities abroad is, the higher the degree of internationalization
UNCTAD; Van Tulder, R. and Ruigrok, W.	1996	Corporate level	*Transnationality index*: is calculated as the average of the ratio of foreign assets to total assets, foreign sales to total sales and foreign employment to total employment
Van den Berghe, D.	2001		

Author	Year	Level	Description
Gestrin, M., Knight, R.F. and Rugman, A.M.	1999	Corporate level	*Templeton global performance index*: one-year measure of returns on foreign assets, one-year measure of foreign operating margins, three-year measure of returns on foreign assets, three-year measure of foreign operating margins
Montgomery, D.B. and Yip, G.S.	2000	Industry and corporate level	Domestic, international, multinational and global firm: level of international revenues and of product standardization
Ruigrok, W. and Wagner, H.	2000	Corporate level	Number or proportion of non-nationals (of the country of origin) on the board of the MNE; operating costs to total sales
Kearney, A.T.	2001	National level	*Communication technology* (e.g. percentage of population online), *personal contact* (e.g. data on international travel), *trade in goods and services* (e.g. changing share of international trade) and *capital flows* (e.g. inward/outward direct foreign investment)
van den Berghe, D.	2001	Corporate level	*Operations*: TSI, TASI, Sullivan index, etc. *Ownership*: Number or proportion of shares owned by foreigners; number of foreign stock markets an MNE is listed on; use of international accounting standards *Orientation*: managers' conception, psychic dispersion of international operations, top managers' international experience *Performance*: return on assets, sales, equity or investments, ratio of foreign profits to total profits, cost of sale to total sales
Parvatiyar, A.	2001	Company level	Global players, global transitionals and global aspirants

Table 2.4 Dimensions and indicators of globalization according to the literature

Author(s)	Globalization indicators and concepts
	Integration
Perlmutter (1969)	A firm's attitude towards the world (EPRG); geocentric view represents the global company
Leontiades (1985)	The more integrated and rationalized the flow of tasks, the more global the strategy
Porter (1986a,b)	Global integration needs a configuration of the value chain
Doz (1986)	Integration
Martinez and Jarillo (1989, 1991)	Mix of integrative devices, i.e. coordination mechanisms; distinction between formal (centralization, formalization, planning, output control, behavioural control) and informal mechanisms (lateral relations, informal communication, organizational culture)
Bartlett and Ghoshal (1990)	Internal coordination necessary to practice integration and differentiation at the same time
Kobrin (1991)	Intra-firm trade, technological intensity
Morrison and Roth (1992)	Presence of competitors in all key international markets measured by level of international linkages (= extent of industry's international trade in relation to market size) and level of integration
Bennet and Dahlberg (1993)	Transcendation of geographic and national loyalty barriers for meeting needs
Tully (1994); Fraedrich, Herndon and Ferrell (1995); Tomlinson (1991); Parker (1998)	Converging 'global' culture

Reference	Description
Naisbitt (1994); Knoke (1996); Davidow and Malone (1992)	High telecommunication standards providing global access to information, products and markets
Robertson (1995)	The glocalization approach
Parker (1998)	Transcendation of internal boundaries (values, functions)
Millman (1999)	Converging technologies (intra- and inter-company communication and information flow); global-minded top management, experience of setting up global sourcing partnerships; integrated manufacturing, assembly and commercial operations across two or more regions
Wilson (1999)	Coordinated procurement and decision-making process
Kleinert et al. (2000)	Horizontal and vertical integration of companies, observed from an economic point of view (scale effects, price differentiation, etc.)
Montgomery and Yip (2000)	Global integration and centralization to realize the demand for global contracts, service, quality, prices, etc.
Birkinshaw, Toulan and Arnold (2001)	Country-based sales organization, matrix arrangement or customer-focused organization (with rising level of globalization)
Wilson et al. (2001)	The greater the transferability of corporate brand image worldwide, the easier the development of global reach

Standardization

Reference	Description
Levitt (1983)	Worldwide product standardization (e.g. because of increasing homogenization of tastes and market structures)
Swimme (1984)	Development of a uniform global community
Morrison and Roth (1992)	Worldwide product standardization (scale economies)
Nunnenkamp et al. (1994)	Development of uniform regulations and policies in specific regions (e.g. European Union) facilitates globalization
Montgomery and Yip (2000)	Level of international revenues and of product standardization

Table 2.4 (Continued)

Author(s)	Globalization indicators and concepts
	Interdependence
Hout *et al.* (1982)	Interdependence, interpreted as interdependent management for achieving synergies across a company's activities; global volume
Hamel and Prahalad (1985)	Cross-subsidization
Kobrin (1994)	Positive relationship between mindsets (e.g. geocentric) and internationalization
Parker (1998)	General political shifts (e.g. privatization, alleviated tax and trade policies, etc.) influence the globalization process; transcendation of external boundaries (use of IT)
Kleinert *et al.* (2000)	Factor price theory => the greater the differences in factor prices, the more intensive the operations abroad; extent of market imperfection as basis for the decision to produce in a foreign country or not
Montgomery and Yip (2000)	Domestic; international, multinational and global firm
	Differentiation
Porter (1986)	National differentiation
Hamel and Prahalad (1985)	Broad product/service portfolio and product varieties as key point
Martinez and Jarillo (1989, 1991)	Integration and differentiation must be reached simultaneously
Kahn (1995)	Theory of multiplication of cultural differences through globalization
	Centralization
Millman (1999)	Centralized purchasing decision making
Montgomery and Yip (2000)	Global integration and centralization to realize the demand for global contracts, service, quality, prices, etc.

federation of assets and responsibilities (cf. Ghoshal and Bartlett, 1998). Companies in this category pursue a strategy of direct investment in many countries, differentiation and national responsiveness (see also Martinez and Jarillo, 1989, pp. 504f.); the geographical identification is the host country's nationality (Heenan and Perlmutter, 1979). Autonomy is the multidomestic strategies' heart (Beamish *et al.*, 2000, p. 143); products are developed in the home market, then only the product's technology and skills are transferred to affiliates for local adaptation;

2 The second category is defined as international, geocentric or global-transitional (to use Parvatiyar and Gruen's, 2001, terminology). Here, companies are characterized by a centralization of control (the 'centralized hub' of Bartlett and Ghoshal, 1989, pp. 49ff.; Ghoshal and Bartlett, 1998), standardization of product design, process technologies – that is, not taking into account the difference of locations. The firm identifies itself as a company with high authority in the single regional headquarters with collaboration between subsidiaries. It undertakes business in two or more countries, where the culture and organizational structures are similar to those of the home country/headquarters. Centralization and standardization are the most important dimensions in this category (see Hordes, Clancy and Baddaley, 1995; Parker, 1998, pp. 50f; Sera, 1992).

What can be demarcated clearly in this category as a kind of sub-category of internationalization is regionalization ('regiocentric'; see Heenan and Perlmutter, 1979; Kutschker and Schmid, 2002). Regionalization includes worldwide growth of FDI and foreign trade, but at the same time a strong concentration in few countries (especially OECD-countries and triade countries). This is valid for the macroeconomic as well as the microeconomic perspective (see for example Van Tulder and Ruigrok, 1996);

3 The third category is described as global, complex-global, transitional/transnational, or as a global player. The challenge companies face in this category is the simultaneous response to (1) local needs, and (2) integration because of economic forces towards globalization (see for example Bartlett and Ghoshal, 1989, pp. 49ff.; Beamish *et al.*, 2000, p. 163; and Martinez and Jarillo, 1989, p. 505). The operational focus is diverse but with interdependent perspectives, led by flexible coordination (cf. description of 'transnational strategy' in Ghoshal and Bartlett, 1998) and functioning as a network of

horizontal decision making (Beamish *et al.*, 2000, p. 159). The aim is to sustain competitiveness and flexibility as well as organizational learning and innovation. The issue of a global strategy is where to achieve the best combination of technology, quality and cost. The headquarters and subsidiaries identify themselves as parts of a worldwide entity, and affiliates may also obtain worldwide product mandates. According to Parker (1998, p. 51), one way for achieving this category is to become a worldwide symbol (that is, the product as symbol); another is to become a stateless organization known for its specialized products but not for its nationality (see also Hu, 1992, who presents the possibility of measuring the extent of statelessness; already described earlier in this chapter, p. 29).

According to the literature and empirical experience, it must be assumed that not many companies will fall into the transnational or complex global category, because it is difficult to satisfy both demands, local adaptation and global integration, at once. Therefore, it may be better to divide the last category into two: one category where companies have already reached global integration and coordination, but not yet simultaneously local adaptation; and a second category where companies have reached both. However, as the classification used in this work will be developed from the empirical dataset, more or fewer categories may arise than the literature suggests. Therefore, the theoretically discussed categories build the basis for our classification, but are not considered as exclusive.

An approach that must also be mentioned at this point is Hedlund's (1986) heterarchy concept of a modern MNC. The heterarchical company differs from the geocentric company in having many different kinds of centres, subsidiary managers are given a strategic role, and coupling occurs between single organizational units. This approach also points to the normative coordination discussed in the theoretical framework as characterizing global companies. The term heterarchy itself describes a system's organization, which is characterized by self-regulation, a leadership role in the sense of creating visions, and 'multi-centredness' for example. This approach differs from the classic hierarchical considerations regarding strategy and structure. Persons, personalities and competences outweigh the positions in the hierarchical approach and the flow of communication is maximized.

This approach, therefore, also provides important indicators of corporate globalization that were not taken into consideration in the other studies discussed earlier in this chapter.

The classification presented above seems to unite most theoretical definitions of globalization into a harmonic explanatory approach. However, ambiguity and some blurring also exist: for example, Daniels and Radebaugh (1992, p. G-21) use the terms transnational and multinational synonymously. The definition of Levitt (1983) that global firms are those with global strategies that realize economies of scale from worldwide integration and standardization, and that of Hamel and Prahalad (1985) that efforts to balance worldwide standards with demands for localization of products and services is a global strategy, exactly what Yip (1992, p. 10) calls multilocal and Phatak (1992) as well as Ashkenas *et al.* (1995) call glocal. Another term coming to mind when analysing the literature is *denationalization*, which is sometimes confounded with globalization as it reflects the tendency to boundlessness. But this term originated from a political-legal discussion and means the change of tasks and behaviour of nation states. Processes cannot be tied in those states (cf. Kutschker and Schmid, 2002, p. 162).

The different dimensions (centralization versus decentralization and so on) emerging from all the different definitions of being global are examined, and an overview of the representative and non-representative ones characterizing globalization is given in Table 2.5.

Global companies are expected to show a distinctive occurrence of interdependence, integration and coordination as well as certain, if any, occurrence of centralization and standardization. National differentiation is seen as typical for multinational companies, but it can be of importance when considering a complex global (that is,

Table 2.5 Summary of findings in the literature

Representative	Non-representative
• Interdependence	• Market-by-market adaptation (= localization)
• Integration	• National differentiation
• Coordination	
• Centralization	• Geography
• Standardization	

transnational) company, which loads not only on integration and interdependence but at the same time on national differentiation. Geography is used to characterize internationally operating companies. This represents the summary of theoretical findings which were also included in the definition development presented in Chapter 1. Therefore, the definitions are not replicated at this point.

The propositions and hypotheses developed are based on the theoretical framework and will be presented as accumulated in the final section of the chapter, Research issues.

Customer-relationship management

Global customer management is a subarea of customer-relationship management (CRM), and therefore shares a lot of basic principles and starting points with CRM. This is why it is important to discuss selected basic elements of CRM in order to understand the mechanisms of GCM. Customer-relationship management enhances marketing productivity through increases in efficiency and effectivity. Increased efficiency, for example, can be reached through customer retention or integration of the customer to raise his activity level. Effectivity on the other hand is supported by the adequate selection of customers and by optimal and individual means of addressing their needs. This pursuit of effectivity clearly shows that not all customers should be addressed because not all are on the one hand profitable for the supplier, and not all can benefit from the supplier's offers and competencies.

Selection of customers is therefore essential in each stage of the relationship life-cycle; that is, within the customer acquisition phase, the customer retention phase and the customer recovery phase (Bruhn, 2001). A company's challenge lies in the definition of customer selection criteria: should the company draw on quantitative criteria (for example, profit, quantitative customer value) or qualitative criteria (for example, reference value), and should it use static or dynamic methods to calculate the customer value such as customer-oriented contribution-margin accounting, portfolios (both static methods) or the customer lifetime value (CLV, dynamic). CRM can only be successful if the costs caused by CRM strategies and programmes are balanced by profitable customers that appreciate the CRM offers.

Customer segmentation and selection is therefore found as a strategically important feature in each CRM and relationship-marketing[14] approach; as in, for example, the model of Parvatiyar (2001) or the CRM approach of Rapp (2000) (Figures 2.3 and 2.4). Parvatiyar's work is a general framework for organizing customer-relationship management, linking programme purpose, design and partners with management and governance as well as with performance. This framework is considered to offer a good overview as to why the key account selection features (presented within the formation stage, called 'partners') as well as the adequate programme features, which are influenced (beside other factors, of course) by the level of corporate globalization, are of importance. This strengthens the connection to corporate

Figure 2.3   A general framework for organizing CRM

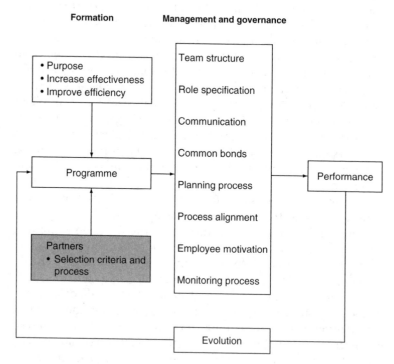

Source: Based on Parvatiyar (2001).

Figure 2.4   CRM approach of Rapp

Stages	Textual partial stages		
1 Customer segmentation	Customer segmentation	Customer processes	Customer profitability
2 Relationship strategies	Focusing	Design of offerings	Programme development
3 Relationship processes and tools	Customer contact	Internal processes	Programme structures
4 Implementation	Temporal planning	Channel management	E-commerce, IT-design
5 Learning from customer relationship	Control of success	Learning transfer	Data-mining

Source: Based on Rapp (2000), p. 40.

globalization and at the same time to the discussion of the globaliza-tion literature.

Rapp's (2000) model pursues the objective of transforming profit-able customers into loyal customers through a holistic CRM approach including customer segmentation and selection, development of differentiated relationship strategies and design of relationship proc-esses and tools, implementation of systematic customer management and efficient learning from customer relationships.

The importance of customer segmentation/selection is clearly shown. This importance also remains if one takes a closer look at one special subarea of customer-relationship management: global customer manage-ment. This research area focuses on the global dimension of customer management, explores differences between national, international and global customer management and adapts concepts and programme designs for global customers. But before a company can segment its customers according to various profitability criteria, it must examine if there are any global customers worth adapting strategies and programmes for. Therefore, the company needs an instrument to classify its customers according to their degree of corporate globalization. At this point, the circle has returned to the original research question of this work: How can companies be classified as global companies? How can this be measured? To be able to answer this question and develop items for the measurement scale, a closer look must be taken at the theory of global customer management.

Global customer management (GCM)

Global customer management is a contemporary research discipline of considerable importance. It is therefore presented in more detail and the connection to corporate globalization is explored.

Recently, international and global enterprises have dealt intensively with GCM, and three different streams addressing the issue of GCM can be identified in the literature: the area of international marketing strategy (see for example Porter, 1986a,b; Prahalad and Doz, 1987; or Yip, 1992), the area of relationship marketing (for example Sheth and Parvatiyar, 2001) and the area of key account management (for example Millman and Wilson, 1995, 1996, 1998; or Wilson; Parvatiyar and Gruen, 2001; Senn, 1999; Wilson, 1999; Wilson *et al.*, 2001; Speare and Reese, 2002). Zupancic and Senn (2000) provide a survey of the importance of GCM in a sample size of 151 global players, examining which activities are really pursued globally. Sales heads the list with 87.4 per cent, followed by customer management with 72.2 per cent. This confirms the increasing relevance of GCM. However, extensive concepts and implementation approaches are still missing. Some authors simply define global customer management as an extended approach to classical key account management (KAM) but with an increased geographical reach. However, geographical reach is not an adequate dimension describing what a global account is. This relates to the definitions of the different categories of globalization and their characteristics described earlier (see Chapter1 and the discussion on delimitations): geography was named as the main characteristic of international companies but as not sufficient for the global category. Of course, an international account may also be of interest for offering such a customer management programme, but the customer's 'category' should be considered in the programme design and offerings. This fact is of importance when talking about the demarcation of international versus global customer management, and relevant definitions are examined in the next sub-section.

Definitions

Global customer management[15] can be defined as the management of relationships with key global customers for long-term profitability (see for example Wilson *et al.*, 2002, p. 43). This definition describes GCM at the strategic level. Zupancic and Senn (2001, p. 7) also structure GCM on a functional and organizational level. According to the functional point of view, GCM designates all activities required to handle global accounts in a worldwide coordinated way. The organizational level includes all persons and entities pursuing global account management functions as well as their integration into the corporate structure. GCM is concerned with marketing 'segments of one', that is, individual customers.

What is not dealt with in this definition is the term 'global customer'. What is a global customer and how can such an account be demarcated from international or multinational customers? Dealing with this issue is important because a key account management programme should be adapted to customers' needs. Global spread represents one influencing factor causing the variation of needs, and therefore key account management can range between different levels of global spread, which then name the respective programme form; for example, national or global account management. The differentiation between programmes is possible by examining their levels on different characterization principles. Wilson *et al.* (2002, p. 103ff.) devise such a framework consisting of four different dimensions of structure: centralized, integrated, decentralized and superimposed. The issues strategic direction, programme delivery and account management are accomplished between these four dimensions and in this way determine the scope of the programme, that is, national, international or global. These four dimensions almost align with findings in the international management literature describing characteristics of international, multinational and global companies, described earlier in this chapter. This fact again clearly shows the direct connection between the level of corporate globalization of the customer company (that is, international, multinational, global, and so on) and the use of a special form of customer management (national, international, global, etc.), adapted to the needs and specificities of the companies within a certain degree. The programme cannot be adapted accordingly if the degree is not known. This shows why the development of a measurement scale is of major importance.

Wilson *et al.* do not differentiate between international or global account management, rather the authors describe different stages of GCM development that companies pass through. This represents another definition opportunity and makes the differentiation between international and global account management unnecessary. This is a major advantage because often a clear demarcation of these terms is impossible. Moreover, according to case studies conducted by Wilson *et al.*, the characteristics presented above seem to occur in parallel with the development stages of GCM programmes. For instance, early GCM tends to be centralized and superimposed over existing structures, whereas the long-term objective is integration of all customer management activites. Centralization is a characteristic of companies operating internationally, which represents the link to international account management. This makes clear that definitional overlaps exist and a sharp distinction of both terms, international key account management (IKAM) and GCM, is not possible. It is also not necessary for the purpose of this research to distinguish between both terms, as it is not the name of the programme that is of importance, but the programme design adapted to the customer's level of corporate globalization.

The differences between traditional versus GCM approaches in marketing were discussed by Wilson *et al.* The relationship marketing approach, focusing on individual customers, customer-centric approaches as well as individually bespoke strategies represent the basis for GCM. Effective GCM needs a more differentiated problem focus than only solving product needs of customers. It also involves process-related needs (that is, incorporating services into the customer's business) as well as facilitation-related needs (dealing with issues such as trust, reduction of uncertainty, development of common culture or congruent systems/structures). These must be adjusted to the characteristics of the global account regarding strategic orientation, capability and focus (Wilson *et al.*, 2002, pp. 85ff.).

To pursue GCM successfully, three issues must be managed: the programme, the relationship and the process (Wilson *et al.*, 2002, pp. 143ff); these activities coalesce to the GCM process. To manage it, an adequate team consisting, for example, of a lead global account manager, senior executives or the CEO, local global customer managers and local service support staff is required. The lead global account manager should be located near the customer's headquarters, the local global customer managers near the remote affiliates, and the support staff as needed in both sites. The local team members deliver the global agreements and provide insights into the customer's remote activities. They should also be responsible for the local implementation and adaptation of global 'promises'.

Approaches

The GCM literature includes a number of different approaches which are now described. The aim of this chapter is the identification of factors and items that can be related to corporate globalization and can therefore contribute to scale development. The approaches are analysed regarding which factors relate (1) to general programme-management problems, (2) to drivers of GCM and, therefore, corporate globalization (a direct relationship is assumed; see Wilson *et al.*, 2002), as well as (3) to actual characteristics of the level of corporate globalization (that is, factors and items needed to be developed for the measurement scale).

Wilson *et al.* (2002) worked out a number of preconditions that enable the effective development and use of GCM programmes. At the core of their model of preconditions is the global mindset that is essential for corporate globalization; for example, to recognize and manage cultural differences. In addition, systems and processes must be integrated and globally coordinated in all value-chain activities to enhance success. This is an important characteristic relating to the level of corporate globalization that can be found in both international business and strategic management literature. The same is true for 'global mindset'. Global account planning as well as adequate reporting systems, supported by communication technology, also contribute to profit. But communication technology is rather a driver than a characteristic of the level of corporate globalization. Another precondition is the reward and compensation system used to motivate and reward the management team. Here, attention must be paid to cultural issues as well as to the impact upon global performance (Wilson *et al.*, 2002, p. 24). Information, communication and knowledge management are also well known as facilitators (drivers) of GCM programmes and of globalization in general. Moreover, for building a strong GCM competence, it is helpful to possess a strong national account management (NAM) capability (if key account management was already implemented on a national basis and advanced to a global level). But this is directly related to programme management. To offer a product with global applications is not enough, one must also provide global value propositions – for example, a consistent pricing strategy providing 'umbrella agreements with country-specific terms and conditions' (Wilson *et al.*, 2002, p. 25).

These are the most important preconditions. However, two are still missing: senior management as well as pan-organizational commitment. Without keeping GCM grounded by the employees, the implementation of a GCM programme is doomed to failure.

Zupancic and Senn (2000) describe GCM according to the same different levels as in key account management (KAM): strategic, functional and organizational. GCM at the strategic level designates the decision to enter and maintain long-term business relationships with selected key accounts; functional GCM includes all activities to handle global accounts coordinated worldwide; organizational GCM incorporates all persons and departments pursuing GCM in the company organization. The implicit assumption is the direct transferability of KAM approaches (supported also by Millman, 1996, and Yip and Madsen, 1996). Intra-company coordination and cooperation are prerequisites for it, and again coordination is a major characteristic. The organizational level mainly relates to programme management, whereas the functional level clearly indicates characteristics of the level of corporate globalization.

Wilson, Speare and Reese (2002, pp. 10ff.) identify three stages in GCM process development: the initiating stage, the development of competencies, and the embedding of GCM processes. The initiating stage contains the following issues: the definition and selection of global accounts, the development of a portfolio approach to the management of the accounts (classified by their degree of geographical spread, operational integration and coordination, their development potential (that is, characteristics of the level of corporate globalization), the involvement of senior executives, and the level of experience (that is, relating to programme-management issues). Developing GCM competencies means developing global terms and conditions, value added services, a single point of contact and local support. This can only be achieved by deploying such processes as supply chain management, network management and information/knowledge management. In addition, these competencies presume a good GCM team and GCM manager as well as organizational flexibility. The last stage indicates the embedding of processes whereby several problems can arise. First of all, customers may utilize GCM programmes only as an opportunity to achieve price concessions instead of cooperation – which is especially the problem when customers are not really global. Secondly, the seller company may lack commitment or global capabilities. Thirdly, inadequate information and communication systems or a lack of global coordination of these systems may cause problems.

Senn (1999) advanced his 9-field matrix from international account management. The central point is the adopted process approach which builds on three process levels, namely the strategic, the operational, and the tactical. 'Strategic' designates the building of long-term relationships, 'operational' the development of worldwide consistent products and services, 'tactical' the provision of a global network infrastructure (see Zupancic and Senn, 2000, pp. 13f.). The first stage, namely setting KAM objectives and strategies, concerns the fields' 'customers', 'solutions' and 'people'. The second stage, the alignment of organizational structures, includes the alignment of 'relationships', 'processes' and 'structures'. Finally, an adequate infrastructure to enable the acceleration of learning processes is required, describing the fields 'knowledge', 'systems' and 'information'. In the present author's opinion, this approach seems to cover customer relationship management issues in general. One focus within this scope is on customers, and therefore also on account selection. Senn and Zeier (2002) present a number of criteria: multinational presence, growth potential (that is, is the key customer growing faster than the market? If it is growing faster, it is a potential global account), access to decision makers, centralized decisions, joint planning with the customer, among the leaders in its market, and significant existing business. But these selection criteria mix items measuring the level of corporate globalization of a customer (that is, centralized decisions), whereas others measure if a global customer should be selected as a global *key* account (that is, significant existing business). Therefore, the approach of Senn and Zeier is regarded as very management-orientated, but as

This model again confirms the importance and necessity of a scale development and its use for GCM. However, no specific suggestions are made how these three customer and supplier types can be identified (that is, measured) and the authors outline only theoretically how the three types are characterized. The global aspirant is seen as a domestic company that expands globally, but has achieved only very little worldwide integration. The global transitional is a multi-domestic firm characterized by a certain degree of centralization of business functions, whereas the global player has integrated all major business functions worldwide and has a high need for world-wide services (Parvatiyar and Gruen, 2001). The description of these types is developed from Perlmutter's basic ideas and Ghoshal and Bartlett's concepts. In this way, the approach shows mainly the same factors characterizing the level of corporate globalization as found in the international management literature discussed earlier in this chapter.

Goals and reasons for implementation

Arnold, Birkinshaw and Toulan (1999, p. 14) give a short review of the common goals of GCM: increasing sales, increasing customer lock-in, fighting-off competitors, reducing price arbitrage and developing new products together with customers. From these aims it can be derived that GCM represents a customer-centric structure within a company and must be seen as an additive form of sales unit.

The reasons for implementation are closely associated with the GCM goals. GCM programmes tend to be implemented for different reasons (cf. Zupancic and Senn, 2000): first, as a reaction to customers' requirements for internationally coordinated support; second, as proactive reaction before customers demand GCM; and out of a continuous development of their key account management to international and then global account management.

The first case occurs when customers are really global and demand a globally integrated product/service offering from their suppliers. Here, it is important to be able to define the degree of globalization of customers in order to decide on the composition of the account management programme features. Proactive reactions also require an assessment of the customer's degree of globalization (that is, assignment of customers to their current stage in the globalization process), since only then can GCM be initiated at an optimal time – initiating GCM too early does not enhance competitive advantage, but risks wasting resources. Therefore, the development of KAM to GCM must be initiated by global customers, the supplier's global orientation alone is not sufficient for GCM success.

Benefits and costs

GCM can help to prevent suboptimization and rivalry between affiliates in different countries and can add to economies of scale and scope. Moreover, companies pursuing GCM can participate in their customers' international growth, and in this way comprehensive learning organizations develop. GCM offers one way to practice intra-organizational relationship management across borders and, simultaneously, increases switching costs for the contractor. But there are also costs to be taken into account: cost and risk of structural changes to one's own organization, acquisition and training costs for GCM managers, development of adequate communicational structures and controlling instruments for coordination as well as increasing fixed costs because of new organizational structures (see Yip and Madsen, 1996, p. 38ff.).

Developing successful customer-management strategies means adjusting strategies and programmes to customers' demands. A possible imbalance in a customer–vendor relationship can result in a benefit to one party through having a more powerful control position and the ability to put pressure on the other partner. A certain dependence arises which influences the account performance – according to the resource dependency view and investigations of Birkinshaw, Toulan and Arnold (2001). But as a balanced relationship and high account performance are goals of the customer-management approach, the necessity for establishing GCM on an equal customer–vendor basis becomes clear. Moreover, a known degree of globalization supports the decision as to which key accounts shall be selected for a GCM programme or indeed whether any adequate account exists (otherwise much money could be saved by not investing in ineffective and inadequate programmes).

Key accounts

When GCM is implemented, the question arises as to what constitutes a global account. A definition is given by Zupancic and Senn (2000) that: 'global accounts are such international (potential) accounts, who have strategic importance for a company and who demand from their suppliers a consistent or coordinated support for determined countries or worldwide'. These accounts have different needs according to their degree of corporate globalization and can/should be segmented according to their LoCG. However, companies often equate these different 'types' of customers.

According to the literature, such global accounts have integrated and coordinated strategies as well as products/services (see for example Wilson *etal.*, 2001, p. 9; and Wilson, Speare and Reese, 2002, pp. 1f.) which they demand also from their suppliers. In this sense, the supplier has to make specific investments in those relationships, which leads to interdependence of both parties. Wilson *etal.* (2002, p. 95) summarize the vital factor of global customer management programmes: 'GCM strategies are essentially concerned with creating value for and with global clients through the coordination of sales, services, operations, logistics, information systems, and ultimately strategic integration worldwide'.

The precondition of a really global customer is of importance insofar as the implementation of a global agreement with a non-global customer will rarely exceed a global pricing agreement. So, treating non-global accounts globally is expensive and counterproductive. Wilson, Speare and Reese (2002, p. 2) postulate that the degree to which companies' operations are coordinated internationally will directly impact upon their ability to act either as global customers or suppliers. This requires that the degree of coordination increases during the development of a company's operations from national to international, regional and global.

National companies can well serve national accounts, but lack of international presence and cross-border coordination makes it impossible to serve global customers. An international company's ability to care for global customers is in turn restricted by its geographical spread, as well as its lack of local capability. At the regional stage, each region has probably identified its own accounts and, therefore, no integrated coordination of activities is possible. But as competition in the market is no longer between companies, but between supply chain networks, integration and coordination of activities are essential. The global stage is characterized by high organizational complexity and cultural diversity at the same time, and can only be balanced through integration and coordination of activities, information management, operations and so on. The same differentiation is drawn at the customer's side, where it is important to notice that each account type must be served differently (*ibid.*, pp. 3ff.).

Selection of key accounts

Managing the programme is one issue in GCM, which contains the implementation of effective global account selection and deselection processes. Therefore, deciding on potential accounts is one of the first important steps in programme management.

Most authors speak of key account selection as a whole; that is, the criteria 'global spread' or 'degree of globalization' are always included among the many selection variables (for example, growth potential or profitability). However, according to this author's opinion, it is more efficient to first analyse if a company has global customers at all. Secondly, the customers already identified as a target group for GCM should be analysed according to their growth potential and potential revenues, that is, the classical selection criteria described earlier in this chapter. This can save resources if the result is 'no global customers' who would need/demand GCM. Then no GCM planning or programme design need be carried out.

A two-step selection process works as follows. First, customers are segmented according to their 'coverage' – international, multi-national, global or transnational. This is important as customers require different support depending on the range of their operational activities. A decision must then be taken as to which level of customers is treated with specific key account management programmes. Many companies simultaneously pursue a national, international and global KAM (see for example Hilti Group, Corporate Case Study, 2002), whilst others have only national or global customers. The second step marks the decision as to which key account to choose within a certain level, since in deciding on global accounts it must be taken into consideration that not every global customer is or should be at the same time a global key account.

The first step in this approach is the objective of this work, whilst the second is frequently discussed in the literature to which the reader is referred (for example Senn and Zeier, 2002; Wilson *et al.*, 2001, 2002; Yip and Madsen, 1996). Only a variety of selection criteria are presented here for a short overview[16] (Wilson, 1999, p. 32) to highlight the mixture of criteria for key account selection in the literature:

- *Quantitative criteria*: turnover, growth potential (e.g. company is growing faster than the market => global account; Senn and Zeier, 2002), global presence, central purchasing, global capability, operational fit and demand for global service; a substantial part of the worldwide transaction volume with the transaction partner is done in other countries than the home country (cf. Kulessa, Frank and Stangl, 1999, p. 22); integrated manufacturing, assembly, commercial operations.
- *Qualitative criteria*: degree of strategic fit, global mindset, value opportunity, potential for relational closeness and senior management commitment; expectations of coordinated supply and a global account support service worldwide (cf. Millman, 1999, p. 3), access to decision makers, joint planning with the customer (cf. Senn and Zeier, 2002).

The quantitative criteria are used mostly in the early stages of a supplier's GCM development, whereas the qualitative criteria are designed for the late stages and need more experience. Both categories include characteristics of 'global', which have already been presented in detail in the definition of what constitutes a 'global company'.

Another classification system of selection criteria is presented by Wilson *et al.* (2002) who separate the criteria according to operational and relational factors. However, the operational factors (for example, future sales potential, increasing global expenditure or most profitable customer) mostly correspond to the quantitative criteria and the relational factors (for example, the potential for developing close buyer–supplier relationships or for strategic alignment) mostly meet the qualitative ones.

It is necessary to notice at this point that the criteria chosen for key account selection depend of course on the product the company is selling and should be adapted to each specific company. The enumeration of criteria given above is of course not complete.

Connection of globalization and GCM

Globalization is not only a subject in international business, economics or social sciences, but also in marketing. As markets globalize, new forms or concepts to market products and services are needed. Global marketing is the general approach to this challenge. Relationship marketing[17] focuses on customer satisfaction, loyalty and retention, and the management of relationships is the key success factor of today's companies. One element is the management of key accounts (KAM). Because of globalization, KAM was set into the global context: global account management.[18] Here, the 'complexity of the selling process, the strategic importance of the customer and the demands for resources with which to manage the relationship all increase' (Wilson, Speare and Reese 2002, p. 32) the higher the level of globalization. Global account management is a trend and for many companies the 'question is not whether to initiate GCM programs, merely when' (*ibid.*, p. 9). GCM programmes are utilized widely if a firm's customers start to globalize; customers more and more demand *global* account management. This awareness is underlined by Montgomery and Yip (2000) who conducted a study which showed a strong relationship between customers' demands for GCM and suppliers' use:

Customer demands from global suppliers

- Single point of contact simplifying negotiation and management of the relationship.
- Coordination of resources for serving customers.
- Uniform prices – unless there is cost justification (e.g. transportation, order size, etc.), not for market variations (e.g. higher price in one market because of supply and demand).
- Uniform terms of trade (e.g. in volume discounts, transportation changes, overhead, etc.).
- Centralized purchasing: standardization of products and services as well as consistency in service quality and performance (e.g. economies of scale, consistent rebates, etc.).

Suppliers' necessary implementations

- Global account managers – typically located in the customer's headquarters' country.
- Support staff – mostly based at supplier's own headquarters.
- Revenue/profit measures on a global basis.

- Reporting processes on all aspects of a global account (including e.g. customer satisfaction and use of services in different geographies).
- Customer information (reporting results in intensive information about the customers).
- Personnel evaluation on a global basis.
- Incentives and compensation also seen on a global basis.
- Customer councils or panels.
- Need to avoid internal competition.

Yip and Madsen (1996) developed a framework of globalization for orientation in GCM, identifying eight drivers of globalization which require the implementation of GCM programmes. These drivers are: global customers, global channels, transferable marketing, lead countries, global economies of scale, high product development cost, fast-changing technology, and globalized competitors. Again, 'global' customers are seen as one key factor for GCM. However, to determine global customers, it is necessary to be able to operationalize and measure this construct, 'global'. Again, globalization and GCM as an instrument are highly connected. For successful implementation of GCM, organizational as well as strategic operations are essential (Figure 2.6), but because of the many different influencing factors, the configuration of GCM is not simple (cf. Zupancic and Senn, 2000, p. 9).

As GCM has been introduced in a highly complex and globalized business world, which indicates a high rate of change, traditional formal marketing approaches are no longer adequate to respond to the changing requirements. Wilson, Speare and Reese (2002) present a model of GCM relationship stages. The authors presume a process development from pre-GCM to early-, mid-, partnership- and, finally – the longer the relationship is continued – to synergistic-GCM. Each key account relationship passes through these stages. At the first stage (=pre-GCM), the relationship is assumed to be between the global account manager and the global purchasing officer (or team) at the customer's headquarters (see Wilson, Speare and Reese, 2002, pp. 52ff.). The relational distance is relatively high, and organizational complexity and cultural diversity rise constantly from the pre- to the synergistic-GCM stage. Challenges at this level are to define if the customer is globally coordinated, what the global business potential is, and so on. The pre- and early-GCM stages are the ones where the

Figure 2.6   Framework for global account management

Industry globalization drivers	Organization response	Implementation
Global/regional customers	Organization structure Management processes People Culture	Consistent world wide sevice
Global/regional channels		One point of contact
Transferable marketing Lead countries	**Need for global account management**	Partnering with customers
Global economies of scale	Global strategy	Outsourcing for customers
High product development cost	Global market participation	Global account management structure
Fast-changing technology	Global services	Compensation and incentive systems
Competitors globalized	Global value chain	Uniform purchasing and pricing
	Global marketing	
	Global competitive moves	

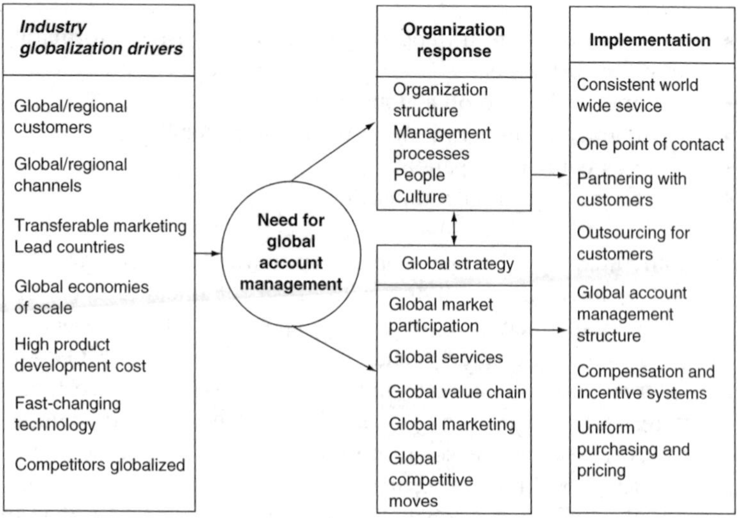

Source: Yip and Madsen (1996), p. 25.

measurement tool can be used most effectively, because there the basic decision about the incorporation or rejection of a customer as a global account (that is, key account segmentation) is made. In the mid-GCM stage an increased level of trust as well as relationship-specific adaptations can be observed, also representing the testing stage of a relationship. In the partnership stage both parties perceive the strategic importance of the relationship, and in the synergistic-GCM stage the parties create joint value in the market.

Wilson, Speare and Reese (2002, pp. 35ff.) also argue that a new strategy development process is necessary to model GCM programmes and to get a grip on the modified conditions because of globalization issues. The authors therefore develop a non-linear, but continuous, incremental, opportunistic and political model of GCM strategy development. This model contains the following stages: exploration, proposal, test, transformation, consolidation and review/reorientation process elements. The whole process is carried by the strategic intent, which can be compared to the 'vision' in the transaction marketing approach. One's own company's as well as the customer's level of corporate globalization influence the variable 'strategic intent', which again shows the connection between GCM and the level of corporate globalization very clearly.

In the present author's opinion, especially the areas of account selection (as already described) and offered benefits are affected by the globalization issues. These are the critical points where companies gain or lose money. The benefits offered depend heavily on the accounts chosen. For example, pricing agreements must be handled totally differently when the customer operates only nationally or when a global customer demands globally consistent prices. Therefore, key account selection is the chosen research area where the development of the measurement scale can bring great advantages. One proposition is already upcoming when connecting both research disciplines: GCM can be used effectively for customers belonging to the simple global or complex global (that is, transnational) categories.

The connection of GCM and globalization also enables consideration of the extent to which companies with different degrees of globalization use various forms of key account management. It can be stated that most companies mix national, international and global KAM, and often pursue all three forms in parallel without clearly distinguishing different types of customers.

Research issues

After completing our literature review, it is necessary to consolidate the research aspects presented so far to formulate propositions and to describe the starting points (that is, dimensions) for the development of the scale's item battery. The propositions are listed below, followed by the dimensions and possible operationalizations (partly taken from theory and partly from empirical studies; examples of the literature from which the hypotheses were derived are presented in Table 2.6).

Dimensions for the measurement and categorization of companies

Possible principles found in the literature as characteristics of globalization are summarized below. Their operationalization can be found partly in literature and is also presented. As already described, most existing measurement approaches measure the LoCG as 'geography bound', that is, the measurement unit is always set in a geographic

Hypothesis 1a: One classified group of companies will be characterized by high global integration and low local adaptation, another group by parallel realization of global integration and localization.
Hypothesis 1b: Most companies can be assigned to the first category, but few are found in the second group realizing global integration and localization in parallel.
Hypothesis 2:   One group of companies will be characterized by high local adaptation and decentralization.
Hypothesis 3:   Coordination increases during the development of a company's operations from national to global.
Hypothesis 4:   The degree of corporate globalization is not dependent on the kind of industry the company operates in.
Hypothesis 5:   GCM is mostly used within firms pursuing global integration and localization in parallel.
Hypothesis 6:   It is assumed that a typical order exists, in which the value chain activities are globalized.

Table 2.6   The hypotheses linked to the literature

Hypotheses	Literature supporting the hypotheses
Hypothesis 1a	• Porter (1986a,b) • Doz (1986) • Hamel and Prahalad (1985) • Leong and Tan (1993) • Martinez and Jarillo (1989) • Bartlett and Ghoshal (1989) • Beamish *et al.* (2000)
Hypothesis 1b	• Leong and Tan (1993)
Hypothesis 2	• Ghoshal and Bartlett (1998) • Heenan and Perlmutter (1979) • Martinez and Jarillo (1989) • Beamish *et al.* (2000)
Hypothesis 3	• Wilson (1999) • Montgomery and Yip (2000)
Hypothesis 4	• Kutschker and Schmid (2002)
Hypothesis 5	• Montgomery and Yip (1999)
Hypothesis 6	• Porter (1986a,b) • Leontiades (1985)

form such as the ratio of *foreign* sales to total sales, the ratio of *foreign* subsidiaries to total subsidiaries, and so on. But the single use of the geographic unit as the measurement unit is not adequate, because geography is mostly a characteristic of international and not specifically global companies. Therefore, the measurement developed in this work is not only based on geography units, but on strategy integration and the process of coordination. The scale reflects the following four main units: corporate orientation, existing corporate strategy, processes, and people. The first unit includes respondents' understanding of globalization as well as the understanding of corporate orientation regarding globalization. The former implies an anchor statement (agreement/disagreement) on what represents globalization, the latter represents firms' beliefs in globalization. The second unit, corporate strategy, covers the integration of activities (that is, which of certain strategies are adapted or not adapted, and which of the given statements represent companies' strategies). The third unit, process, implies the question of how a firm conducts processes (that is, which of the given processes have already been established in the company). The fourth unit, people, includes attitudes, values and activities of employees.

- **Standardization**
  - (a) Of product/ service;
  - (b) Of process technologies;
  - (c) Of strategies;
  - (d) Of organizational culture,
    - Degree to which the culture equals the 'normed' home-country culture;
  - (e) Of organizational structure,
    - Degree to which the organizational structure equals the 'normed' home-country structure;
  - (f) Of 'knowledge' through joint knowledge-development programmes, for example;
  - (g) Low degree of differences in markets, consumer needs, etc. between countries;
  - (h) Coordination (=> according to Martinez and Jarillo (1991) the mix of integrative devices is a sub-variable of integration). Formal mechanisms are:

– Centralization (the extent to which the locus of decision making lies in higher levels of the chain of command;

– Formalization (the extent to which policies, rules, job descriptions, etc. are written down in manuals and other documents leading to standard routines);

– Planning (strategic planning, budgeting, establishment of schedules, intended to guide and channel the activities of independent units);

– Output control (evaluation of files, records and reports submitted by the organizational units to corporate management);

– Behavioural control (direct, personal surveillance of the subordinate's behaviour);

(i) Communication and IT technology standard.

- **Interdependence**
  (a) Cross-subsidization,
      – Use of financial resources gained in one part of the world for fighting competition in another part;
  (b) Organizational learning,
      – Share of intangible assets;
      – Share of knowledge;
  (c) Competitive position in one country is dependent on the one in other countries.

- **Integration**
  (a) Worldwide integrative strategy;
  (b) Worldwide integrated products;
  (c) Worldwide brand distribution,
      – Transferability of corporate brand image worldwide (=> the greater, the easier to develop global reach);
  (d) Worldwide mindset of managers;
  (e) Worldwide working experience;
  (f) Worldwide vision;
  (g) Worldwide integrated information;
  (h) Informal coordination mechanisms;
      – Lateral relations (direct contact among managers of different departments that share a problem, temporary or permanent task forces, teams, committees, integrative departments, etc.);
      – Informal communication (creation of a network of informal and personal contacts among managers across different units

of the company, corporate meetings and conferences, management trips, personal visits, transfers of managers, etc.);
– Organizational culture (process of socialization of individuals by communicating to them the way of doing things, the decision-making style and the objectives and values of the company).

- **Differentiation**
  - (a) National adaptation of products/services;
  - (b) National adaptation of strategies;
  - (c) National responsiveness,
    - Exploitation of local market opportunities;
    - Self-sufficiency of assets and capabilities;
    - National development and retaining of knowledge.
- **Centralization vs Decentralization**
  - (a) Of control over assets, capabilities, purchasing, strategy, knowledge, operational acivities, etc.;
  - (b) Decision-making authority lies within the HQ;
  - (c) Local profit and loss responsibilities, local decisions, procurement and resources; local governance of affiliates; etc.
- **Resources**
  - (a) Global presence (geography bound),
    - Ratio of foreign assets to total assets;
    - Ratio of foreign sales to total sales;
    - Ratio of foreign employment to total employment;
    - Ratio of overseas subsidiaries to total subsidiaries;
  - (b) Global resource allocation,
    - Use of financial resources across HQ and affiliates, independent from which part of the company the resources stem from;
    - Differences in factor prices as reason of worldwide activities.
- According to **Porter's value chain**, the following corporate activities must also be considered:
  - Purchasing;
  - Manufacturing/ production;
  - Marketing/sales;
  - Service;
  - Research and development;
  - Human resource management;
  - Firm infrastructure (finance, etc.).

This summary includes all possible dimensions and indicators named in the literature as characterizations of global companies. These dimensions and indicators are included in the qualitative interviews to survey how experts characterize a global company and whether these are of little or great importance in practice. The results of these interviews are used to refine the items in Chapter 4.

3
Research Methodology

This research is based on the realism paradigm as its reference framework because this paradigm is characterized by 'confirmatory' theory-building with focus groups or interviews (in this work the expert interview technique is used) and/or theory-testing with structural equation modelling (SEM). Perry (2002) concludes that realism is an 'appropriate paradigm for more business research, especially in marketing'.

Construct measurement

The aim of applied science is to understand and predict real phenomena, and to be able to accomplish this the researcher must refer to a theoretical explanatory approach for each case of problem-setting. All approaches have in common that they specify relationships between abstract concepts or constructs (cf. Sullivan and Feldman, 1979, p. 9); a connection can then be drawn between the theoretical level of analysis and the empirical level of problem-setting through development and use of measuring techniques. These measuring techniques capture observable properties of the respective units of analysis (cf. Werani, 1998, p. 78), and these properties reflect the characteristics of the abstract constructs in use. The observable properties grasped by the measurement are designated as indicators of abstract, unobservable and not directly measurable constructs (cf. Sullivan and Feldman, 1979, p. 9). Therefore, the measurement process can be summarized as the connection of abstract concepts or constructs with empirical, numerically recordable indicators (cf. Carmines and

Zeller, 1979, p. 10; Werani, 1998, p. 78). This definition implies that beneath the explicit theories and hypotheses, a second theory, the so-called auxiliary theory, is often needed. This auxiliary theory defines the relationships between the theoretical and empirical approaches and, therefore, between abstract constructs and observable indicators. The relationships described are also called 'correspondence hypothesis' or 'epistemic correlations' and lead to the operationalization of abstract, hypothetical constructs (see for example Backhaus *et al.*, 1994).

These reflections so far can be summarized with the help of an example taken from the subject of this research: two abstract concepts or constructs, namely the level of corporate globalization and company size, build the theoretical basis. The two constructs are connected to each other in the following form: it is suggested that company site (CS) within a company is causal for the level of corporate globalization (CS-G hypothesis). To be able to test this hypothesis, it is necessary to make both abstract constructs measurable; that is, to operationalize the two constructs through observable indicators. This is done on the basis of the correspondence hypothesis, which in this case states that the company size can be measured by three indicators (cs_1, cs_2 and cs_3) and the level of corporate globalization also by three indicators (g_1, g_2, g_3) (Figure 3.1). The empirical values can be gained, for example, through interrogation of a certain number of informants.

Reliable statements regarding the relationship between the indicators cs_1, cs_2 and cs_3 and the concept of company size, as well as between the indicators g_1, g_2, g_3 and the concept of level of corporate globalization, are *significant*. Otherwise, if the relationships between indicators and constructs are weak or specified in a false way, wrong

Figure 3.1   Measurement process of abstract constructs

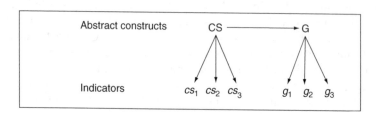

conclusions will be drawn (cf. Werani, 1998, p. 80). To fulfill the request of the applied science described above, namely to understand and predict real phenomena, this work is inseparably connected with the problems of measuring abstract and complex constructs.

The three different elements constituting Figure 3.1 are now presented in detail. The abstract constructs, often also named latent constructs, can have varying degrees of complexity and can be systematized as follows (see also Figure 3.2):

- One-dimensional constructs (cf. Homburg, 1995, p. 64): construct and dimension are equivalent and the observable indicators are directly connected with the construct (dimension);[19]
- Multi-dimensional constructs: include two or more latent dimensions, divided into dimensions of primary and secondary order;

Figure 3.2 Systematization of abstract constructs

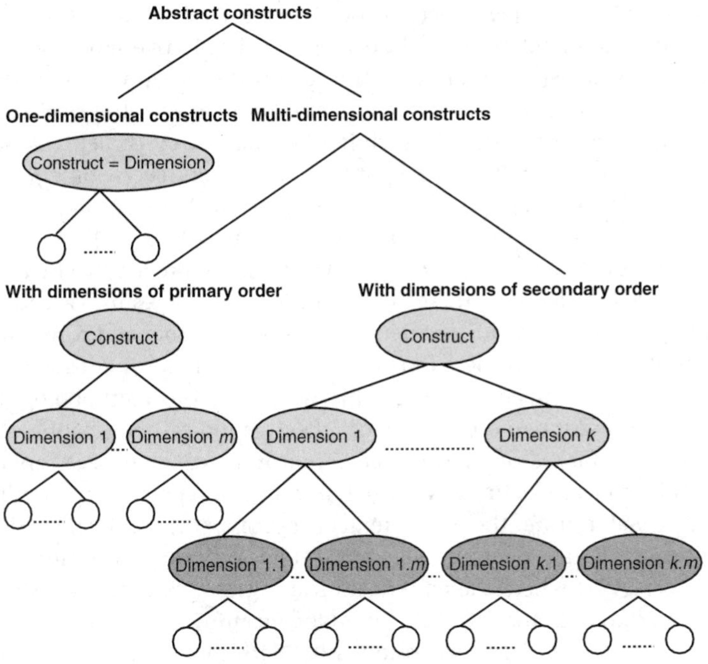

Source: Based on Homburg and Giering (1996), p. 6

primary order means that a construct is operationalized through only one level of latent dimensions and the correspondingly assigned, observable indicators; secondary order means that there exist dimensions that bundle up dimensions below; these single dimensions have the function of indicators, and consequently in secondary order dimensions both observable and non-observable (latent) indicators[20] can arise.

The observable indicators of a construct are the second element to be presented in more detail. The first question to be answered is that of how many indicators are needed to operationalize and measure a construct adequately. This question can be answered by stating that, in general, the researcher gets more precise results if a construct is measured by multiple observable indicators, and Churchill (1979, p. 66) names a variety of reasons why it is of advantage to use multiple indicators. The reasons are not further described here in this overview, and the interested reader is referred to more detailed descriptions in the literature (for example Anderson and Gerbing, 1982; Churchill, 1979).

Two forms of indicators can be distinguished: reflective and formative indicators. Reflective indicators proceed on the assumption that the indicators reflect the characteristics and properties of the construct on which they are based,[21] which implies that the construct is causal for the indicators.[22] If one looks at this causality in reverse order (that is, the construct as a function of its indicators) one speaks about formative indicators (cf. Homburg and Giering, 1996, p. 6).

Our work on the subject of the LoCG development is based on reflective indicators, as these take measurement failures into account, which forms the major difference between reflective and formative indicators. The consideration of measurement failures corresponds better to the pursued aims of this work and the methodological approach used, because the use of reflective indicators is connected with the demand for *unidimensional* indicators, which is necessary to be able to clearly define a construct. If indicators appear as not unidimensional during the measurement process, the problem called 'interpretational confounding' arises (cf. Anderson and Gerbing, 1982, p. 454) where the empirical meaning of a construct does not correspond with the originally intended meaning.

The last element for discussion is the correspondence hypothesis. The underlying assumption of the example illustrated is that the indicators presented are influenced only by the theoretical, abstract constructs – not by any other factors. However, different disruptive factors (cf. Sullivan and Feldman, 1979, pp. 11f; and Werani, 1998, p. 84) can always occur in empirical practice, and can be divided into random and systematic errors.[23] Empirically ascertained indicators therefore not only reflect the true values of the underlying abstract constructs, but also these random and systematic errors.[24] Consequently, the aim is to design measurement models and instruments in such a way that the approximation to the true value is as good as possible.

In connection with this, the problem of the measurement instrument's goodness and the criteria used to determine this goodness has to be mentioned. Generally, the concepts of validity, reliability and objectivity are used to describe a work's quality, and within the validity construct, the researcher distinguishes between content validity, criterion validity and construct validity. Within the 'construct validity', convergence validity, discriminant validity and nomological validity are of importance. For detailed descriptions of the single types of validity, the interested reader is referred to Bagozzi (1994), Hildebrandt (1984), Homburg and Giering (1996) or Werani (1998). Later on in the data analysis section, the author only explains the concepts relevant to the concrete research problem of this work. Within the reliability construct, stability and consistency play a major role (see for example Carmines and Zeller, 1979, pp. 37ff.). Objectivity can be divided into objectivity in carrying out the research, objectivity of analysis and objectivity in the interpretation of results. Moreover, objectivity should be seen as a precondition for achieving validity and reliability.

To ensure and test the validity and reliability of research, different approaches exist which can be divided into first-generation and second-generation criteria. First-generation criteria are based on early psychometric measurement approaches[25] and include:

- exploratory factor analysis
- Cronbach's alpha and
- item-to-total correlations.

All three criteria have different requirements. The literature suggests not one single value as the optimum, but rather that the statements imply a certain range of values. Therefore, the following requirements were chosen:

- Exploratory factor analysis: requires a value ≥ 0.45 of each indicator
- Standardized Cronbach's alpha: requires a value ≥ 0.70
- Item-to-total correlations: if the alpha is too small, the indicators with the lowest correlations are gradually eliminated.[26]

Second-generation criteria are based on a confirmatory factor analysis and contain criteria to test the entire model fit as well as the fit of partial model components. For the entire model fit, the following criteria, also named 'global criteria', can be used:

- *Likelihood-ratio test (χ^2 value) and the quotient of χ^2/df:* the quotient is taken as a criterion because it is not as sensitive regarding the sample size as the likelihood-ratio test; the quotient is a descriptive measure to examine the adjustment and Homburg and Giering (1996, p. 13) request values of ≤ 3.
- *Root-mean-square error of approximation (RMSEA):* is examined with the 'test of close fit' in LISREL (Linear Structural Relationships); a computer programme for carrying out covariance structure analysis; see pp. 85ff.); the H_0 hypothesis that RMSEA ≤ 0.05 cannot be rejected if the *p*-values are *not* significant; values of RMSEA ≤ 0.08 state an acceptable model fit, and values of ≤ 0.05 an excellent model fit (cf. Jöreskog and Sörbom, 1996, pp. 341ff.). Therefore, the minimum requirement is $p \leq 0.08$; moreover, it is tested if the 'test of close fit' shows a value of $p \geq 0.05$, which is a more rigorous criterion (cf. Werani, 1998, p. 109).
- *Goodness-of-fit index (GFI):* corresponds to the coefficient of determination of the regression analysis and ranges analogically between 0 and 1; if the GFI reaches 1, all empirical variances and covariances could have been calculated by the model.
- *Adjusted goodness-of-fit index (AGFI):* this is again a measure for the variance explained by the model and also shows a range of values between 0 and 1; in addition to the GFI, this measure includes 'penalty terms' depending on the number of parameters used

(cf. Backhaus *etal.*, 2000). For both, the GFI and AGFI, values of ≥0.90 are suggested (cf. Homburg and Baumgartner, 1995, p. 170; or Werani, 1998, p. 110).

- *Comparative fit index (CFI)*: shows to what extent the goodness of fit increases by the change from a basic model (formed without any plausibility, all indicator variables are set as independent) to the relevant model (cf. Homburg and Baumgartner, 1995, p. 170). As the relevant model is normally better than the basic model, this criterion is not very rigorous and should only be used supplementarily.

For the test of the partial model components, the approaches named below are used. These criteria include all validity and reliability criteria; that is, a separation between criteria defining the entire model fit of an empirical data set (the global criteria) and the validity/reliability criteria exists. But the fullfilment of the global criteria is necessary to prove the model in detail regarding validity and reliability.

- *Indicator reliability*: shows the share of variance for each observed variable, which is explained by the corresponding latent variable; it is calculated automatically by LISREL and is called 'squared multiple correlation for the ith observed variable' (cf. Jöreskog and Sörbom, 1996, pp. 26f). The range of values is between 0 and 1; 1 is reached if the variance of the measurement error is zero; a small indicator reliability points to the fact that a construct is not adequately grasped by the variable; for sample sizes between $n = 100$ and $n = 400$, most researchers demand a value of ≥0.40 (cf. Homburg, 1995, p. 83).
- *Construct reliability*: a construct must be measured adequately by the entirety of its indicators; this measure is also called 'factor reliability' or 'composite reliability' and is again defined between 0 and 1; values of ≥0.60 are required. For the detailed calculation formula used also in this research, the reader is referred to Homburg and Giering (1996, pp. 10f.).
- *Average variance explained (AVE) of a construct*: shows the goodness of the construct measurement through its entire range of indicators and is normed between 0 and 1; the required value is ≥0.50 (cf. Homburg and Giering, 1996, p. 13). Both the construct reliability and the AVE examine the internal consistency reliability.

- *Confidence test of the factor loadings*: to ensure convergence validity, all factor loadings of the single indicators have to be significantly different from 0; only then can an adequate connection be assumed between the indicators and the construct. When using a single-tail test and a significance level of $\alpha=0.05$, the factor loading is significantly different from zero if the absolute t-value is at least 1.645 (cf. Homburg, 1995, p. 84).
- χ^2 *discrepancy test*: used to evaluate the discriminant validity. The correlation between two indicators is fixed on the value 1; the chi square of the resulting model is then compared to the basic model. The chi square difference between both models is significant (on a significance level of 0.05) if the value is at least the same as results from the theoretical chi square value with one degree of freedom (resulting from the fixation of *one* parameter), that is, 3.841 (cf. Homburg and Giering, 1996, p. 11).
- *Fornell–Larcker criterion*: suggests a comparison of the AVE and the squared correlations of the constructs. Discriminant validity according to Fornell–Larcker is given if the AVE of a construct is larger than each squared correlation of this construct with another construct (cf. Homburg, 1995, p. 85). As this criterion is more rigorous than the discrepancy test, it is suggested for this research as the essential measure.

Table 3.1 summarizes the global and detailed criteria used for our model evaluation and shows the specifications adopted for this work.

The LISREL approach

LISREL (**LI**near **S**tructural **REL**ationships[27]) is a computer program for carrying out *covariance structure analysis*. This analysis belongs to the second generation multivariate techniques and combines the confirmatory factor analysis model (stemming from psychometric theory) with the structural equations model (stemming from econometrics). The aim is 'to explain the structure or pattern among a set of latent (i.e. unobserved/theoretical) variables, each measured by one or more manifest (i.e. observed/empirical) and typically fallible indicators' (Diamantopoulos, 1994, p. 223). It can be specified to what extent the posited structure is congruent with the empirical data.

Table 3.1   Guidelines used for the evaluation of the LISREL measuring model

Criterion	Specification
1 Global second-generation criteria	
χ^2/df	≤ 3
RMSEA	≤ 0.08
(H_0: RMSEA ≤ 0.05)	($p \geq 0.05$)
GFI	≥ 0.90
AGFI	≥ 0.90
CFI	≥ 0.90
2 Detailed second-generation criteria (measurement model)	
Indicator reliability	≥ 0.40
Construct reliability/factor reliability	≥ 0.60
Average variance explained (AVE)	≥ 0.50
Confidence test of factor loadings ($\alpha = 0.05$)	$|t| \geq 1.645$
χ^2 discrepancy test ($\alpha = 0.05$)	χ^2-discrepancy ≥ 3.841
Fornell-Larcker criterion	AEV (ξ)$> r^2$ ($\xi j, \xi i$), for i$\neq$j

The covariance structure model consists of two major parts (Diamantopoulos, 1994, p. 223): the *measurement* part (operationalization of the latent variables via the manifest ones and provision of information about validity and reliability of the manifest variables), and the *structural* part (determination of relationships between the latent variables and the quantum of unexplained variance). The actual comparison of the theoretical and empirical structure is done by comparing the computed, theoretical covariance matrix with the covariance matrix arising from the empirical data.

What is especially relevant for this work is the *measurement* part of the analysis; that is, to operationalize the latent variables via the manifest variables (for example, LoCG => the principles characterizing corporate globalization => the single items shown in the questionnaire in Appendix 1). However, a short summary is given below to explain the LISREL modelling sequence:[28] (1) model conceptualization, (2) path-diagram construction, (3) model specification, (4) model identification, (5) parameter estimation, (6) assessment of model fit, (7) model modification and (8) model cross-validation (Diamantopoulos, 1994, p. 225). The LISREL approach traces back to Jöreskog and is implemented in the computer program developed by Jöreskog and Sörbom, used in a Windows™ version for this work.

Model conceptualization

The first step includes on the one hand the structural part of LISREL, where the linkages between the latent variables are determined – that is, a theory-based hypothesis system is developed (first level of analysis; cf. Diamantopoulos, 1994, pp. 226f.). Here, the researcher must distinguish between exogenous (that is, variables not explained by the posited model/independent variables) and endogenous (explained by the model) latent variables. On the other hand, it includes the measurement part where the latent variables are operationalized – that is, represented by the manifest variables which are reflective indicators (cf. Diamantopoulos, 1994, p. 227; or Werani, 1998, p. 98). The assignment of the reflective indicators to the latent constructs is based on correspondence hypothesis, which is derived from the auxiliary theory (second level). This second part is relevant for this empirical research.

Path diagram

The second step is the path-diagram construction, a graphical representation of the relationships between all elements constituting the model (Figure 3.3). The measurement model is the one this work focuses on.

The measurement models describe the relations between the latent variables and the indicators with the straight arrows, here representing the factor loadings as these measurement models constitute the confirmatory factor analysis. This work focuses on this part or 'function' of LISREL – the confirmatory factor analysis – as already mentioned, to validate the item battery.[29] But the presentation of the whole LISREL approach as well as the classification where the confirmatory factor analysis fits in enables the reader to get a concise overview of the overall methodological approach used.

Model specification

The mathematical specification of the model can be derived from the path diagram and in general is as follows (Diamantopoulos, 1994, p. 231):

Figure 3.3   Path diagram, including the measurement model

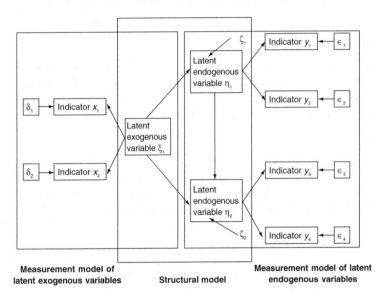

| Measurement model of latent exogenous variables | Structural model | Measurement model of latent endogenous variables |

Source: Backhaus *et al.* (2000), p. 417.

$\eta = B\,\eta + \Gamma\xi + \zeta$ (Structural model)

$y = \Lambda_y\eta + \epsilon$ (Measurement model for latent endogenous variables)

$x = \Lambda_x\xi + \delta$ (Measurement model for latent exogenous variables)

The two equations *y* and *x* are the interesting ones for the purpose of this research, as both characterize the measurement model, that is, the confirmatory factor analysis.

The transfer of the formal model into the LISREL computer language is undertaken through eight matrices. Four of them are coefficient matrices describing the model's paths, the other four are variance-covariance matrices for the exogenous variables and error terms (represented in the mathematical formulation through the 'ζ' residual of the latent endogenous variables, 'ϵ' and 'δ' measurement error specification assigned to *y* and *x*) (cf. Diamantopoulos, 1994, p. 231). The matrices' elements imply a model-based covariance matrix Σ, which must be matched to the empirical sample-based covariance matrix *S*. The covariance matrix builds the basis for the confirmatory factor analysis.

Model identification

The central question in this step is whether the 'information provided by the empirical data ... is actually sufficient to allow for a unique solution of the system of equations containing the model parameters' (Diamantopoulos, 1994, p. 234), that is, to identify the model.

Parameter estimation

The aim is to find values for the parameter metrics. The fitting function *F* should declare the distance (which should be minimized) between the model-based covariance matrix Σ and the empirical sample-based covariance matrix *S* and is written as:

$$f_s(\Lambda, \Phi, \theta_\delta) = F(S, \Sigma((\Lambda, \Phi, \theta_\delta)) \to \min$$

The computer program LISREL® provides several different estimation methods, namely:

- Instrumental variables (IV),
- Maximum likelihood approach (ML),
- Two-stage least squares (TSLS),
- Unweighted least squares (ULS),
- Generalized least squares (GLS),
- Generally weighted least squares (WLS), and
- Diagonally weighted least squares (DWLS).

For detailed description of the individual methods, the interested reader is referred to Jöreskog and Sörbom (1996, pp. 17ff.) and Backhaus *et al.* (2000, pp. 450ff.). The single methods are only described regarding their usability for the analysis and they are interpreted regarding the subject. The choice of method is dependent on the size of the return (for example, the ML approach needs $n > 200$ whereas the ULS approach performs best when having small sample sizes from $n = 100$ to $n = 200$), as well as on the normal distribution (for example, the ML approach should be favoured by multinormal distributions whereas the ULS approach mentioned before is reliable with samples with variance from the normal distribution). Therefore, the connection to the empirical data would suggest the use of the ULS method, as the sample size is $n = 130$ with a normal distribution (see the discussion in Chapter 4 on the measurement dimensions of globalization, p. 142)

The reliability of the parameter estimation can be determined by calculating the 'standard errors' of estimation (if there are large standard errors, the parameters are not reliable) or the multiple square correlation coefficients for each observed and latent endogenous variable as well as for the entire structural equations. This measures the reliability, R, defined as:

$$R = \left(1 - \frac{Error\ variance}{Total\ variance}\right)$$

with $0 \le R < 1$. The nearer the value is to 1, the more reliable are the estimations (cf. Backhaus *et al.*, 2000, pp. 462f.).

Assessment of model fit

After the parameter estimation, the model's goodness of fit has to be assessed. The first assessment must be a logical one; that is, that no values such as, for example, negative variances or correlation coefficients >1 occur. The second assessment is performed through the use of the global and detail criteria described earlier in this chapter, that is GFI, AGFI, CFI, RMSEA, indicator reliability, and so on.

The rejection or acceptance of the model depends on the achievement of the mentioned criteria. First, the global criteria are taken into account. A great variety of suggestions exists according to different authors, which range from model acceptance only if all criteria are completely achieved (100 per cent; see for example Fritz, 1995, p. 143), to rather less demanding requirements. Achievement of 100 per cent is problematic as the single global criteria can show different results according to the particular data situation. The risk is to reject acceptable models rashly. Therefore, the 50 per cent limit suggested by Homburg (1995, p. 85) and, for example, used by Werani (1998, p. 117) is also adopted for this research: 50 per cent of the global criteria must be achieved, the other criteria are only allowed to slightly deviate from the requested specifications.

The same is adopted for the detailed criteria measuring the reliability of the model components, that is, the measurement models. Only if

50 per cent of these criteria are also achieved and the others show only slight deviations, can the measurement models be accepted. As this builds the basis for the entire model, the measurement model must be accepted in order to accept the entire model.

The last steps of the classical LISREL approach are not carried out in this research as the only aim is to validate the measurement scale (for example, model cross-validation is not carried out).

Excursion: exploratory versus confirmatory factor analysis

Exploratory (EFA) and confirmatory (CFA) factor analyses are two major approaches to factor analysis. Factor analysis as a methodological instrument was first used by Spearman in an article in 1904 and was based on Pearson's work on principal axes (see Bollen, 1989, p. 226). Factor analysis tries to 'explain the relationship between a number of observed variables in terms of a single [multiple[30]] latent variable' (*ibid.*). It belongs to the data reduction techniques.

The major difference between the two approaches is that in EFA no model showing the relations of the latent to the observed variables is predetermined. Moreover, the researcher does not define the number of latent variables *ex ante* of the analysis and the measurement errors must not correlate. It is assumed that all latent variables influence all observed variables. Therefore, underidentification of parameters often occurs (cf. Bollen, 1989, pp. 227f.). Opposite to this is the CFA approach, where the model as well as the number of latent variables are defined *ex ante* by the researcher, latent variables may be set to zero (to hold them constant), measurement errors can correlate and parameters must be identified (*ibid.*, p. 228).

EFA is chosen when little is known about the research area and the aim is to detect underlying patterns in the data, whereas CFA is chosen when hypotheses about plausible model structures and relations exist that may be estimated and tested on their fit to the data-set.

The general model for CFA was already included in the description of a general LISREL model, but was probably not recognized as such. Therefore, it is explicitly singled out below:

$$y = \Lambda_y \eta + \epsilon \qquad y, x \dots \text{observed variables}$$
$$x = \Lambda_x \xi + \delta \qquad \eta, \xi \dots \text{latent variables (i.e. } \textit{factors)}$$
$$\epsilon, \delta \dots \text{measurement errors}$$

In our earlier discussion (p. 75), the equation for y was called the measurement model for latent endogenous variables, and that for x the measurement model for latent exogenous variables. For more statistical details of confirmatory factor analysis, the interested reader is referred to Bollen (1989, pp. 233ff.). The individual steps of the approach have already been mentioned in our discussion of the LISREL approach and will not be reiterated further as the only aim of this excursion is clearly to articulate the differences between EFA and CFA for clarification purposes for further analysis and interpretation of our results.

Cluster analysis

Cluster analysis is a classification method used to build groups and belongs to the multivariate method of interdependence analysis. Within groups, affiliates should be alike (homogeneous); that is, show a similar attribute structure. Between groups, affiliates should be as unalike (heterogenous) as possible. Cluster analysis includes all relevant attribute variables at once to build groups. As the cluster method belongs to interdependence analysis, the variables included in this analysis can be dependent on each other. An overview of all relevant steps within the analysis procedure is given in Figure 3.4.

The first step includes the selection of cluster variables. These variables should be supported through theory and should be important for the research question. In this work, the variables selected are the same that were detected as important through the exploratory and confirmatory factor analysis. In addition, these variables are valid across different industries (see Chapter 5, pp. 119 and 148), that is, they are comparable across industries. All requirements are met in this research.

The two major parts that a cluster analysis consists of (Backhaus *et al.*, 2000, pp. 329ff.), and that are included in the next steps of the procedure, are:

1   the selection of the distance or similarity measure and
2   the selection of a clustering procedure.

Step 1: distance versus similarity measure

The starting point of a cluster analysis is the raw data matrix consisting of K objects, which are described by J variables. As the similarity

Figure 3.4   Steps in the clustering procedure

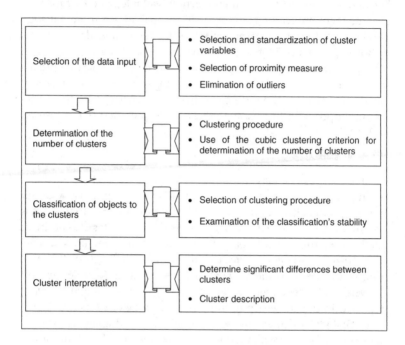

between the objects must be represented by a statistical measure, this raw data matrix is transformed into a distance or similarity matrix that always has a square shape ($K \times K$) (Backhaus *et al.*, 2000, pp. 331f.). It is important to differentiate between distance and similarity measures, because

1 similarity measures reflect the similarity between objects, i.e. the higher the value of this measure, the higher the similarity; whereas the
2 distance measures reflect the dissimilarity between objects, i.e. the higher the distance between objects, the higher the dissimilarity.

There are a number of such proximity measures, and they can also be differentiated regarding the scale level for which they are adequate. For a nominal scale level, Tanimoto's coefficient, Kulczynski's coefficient, the *RR*-coefficient, the *M*-Coefficient or the Dice-coefficient can be used. For a metric scale level, the L-norms (Minkowski metric: City-block distance $= L_1$ norm and Euclidean distance $= L_2$ norm), Mahalanobis' distance or the Q-correlations coefficient are adequate. For detailed information on all measures. Only the Minkowski metric is presented here because it is chosen in the analysis presented in Chapter 4 for the metric scale level of the attributes in this research.

The Minkowski metric can formally be described as (Backhaus *et al.*, 2000, pp. 340f.):

$$d_{k,l} = \left[\sum_{j=1}^{J} |x_{kl} - x_{lj}|^r \right]^{\frac{1}{r}} \tag{3.1}$$

$d_{k,l} =$ distance of objects k and l; x_{kj}, $x_{lj} =$ value of the variable j on object k and l ($j = 1, 2, \ldots J$); and $r \geq 1 =$ Minkowski constant.[31]

The choice of the distance measure significantly influences the order of the objects according to their similarity. Distance measures are adequate if the absolute distance between objects is the subject of interest, that is, if the dissimilarity is greater, the larger the distance between two objects. Similarity measures are adequate if the researcher is interested in the similarity of two profiles, independent from the fact on which level those objects lie (see Backhaus *et al.*, 2000, p. 345). For the research question of this work, it is adequate to use a distance measure: it can be assumed that companies belonging to different groups may have similar profiles on some variables, but the area of interest is how large the differences on the scale are (for example, it is assumed that international and global companies both attach importance to standardization, but to different degrees).

Therefore, Minkowski's distance measure is suggested for use in this research. There is one precondition to fulfil: to be able to use the Minkowski metric, the measuring unit must be comparable. In this research, rating scales from 1 to 7 were used to survey all attribute values of the companies, that is, the precondition for use is met, and therefore this measure is used later on for analysis.

Step 2: selection of clustering procedure

The distance or similarity matrix is the basis for the clustering procedure, which aims to summarize the objects to different groups. The general differentiation of clustering procedures is between monothetic and polythetic approaches. Monothetic approaches only include one variable to group the objects, and therefore such an approach does not support the advantage of the cluster method to use several variables at the same time and cannot be used reasonably in this research. The polythetic approach includes hierarchical, partitional and optimizing procedures as well as procedures based on the theory of graphs.

Partitional procedures start from a given arrangement of the objects in groups. They rearrange the objects between groups according to a given mathematical algorithm until the objective function is optimal (Backhaus *et al.*, 2000, p. 349). These procedures have a greater variability, but are not often used in practice because:

1 the results are influenced significantly by the objective function that rearranges the objects;
2 the selection of the starting partition is subjective and, therefore, also influences the results; and
3 only local but not global optimization can be reached because of technical/computer constraints (*ibid.*, pp. 351f.).

Hierarchical procedures can be divided into agglomerative and divisive procedures. An agglomerative procedure starts with the dispersed partition, that is, the number of groups at the beginning is equal to the number of objects being examined. The single linkage, the complete linkage, the average linkage, the centroid, median and Ward's procedure belong to the agglomerative method, which is mostly chosen for analysis.[32] The divisive procedures function conversely, that is, all objectives are summarized into one group at the beginning and are then separated into several groups during the procedure. Therefore, the decision as to which procedure to use in this research was made for the agglomerative, hierarchical procedure. In Chapter 4 we discuss and justify the method chosen within the hierarchical approach, the *complete linkage method*, also called 'furthest-neighbour method' as it uses the largest distances to group the objectives.

The cubic clustering criterion (CCC) is used to determine the optimal number of clusters, applying it to the number of clusters, starting with 1. The first local maximum gives the indication for the optimal number of clusters (see Jensen, 2001, p. 113).

In the last stage of the cluster analysis, cluster interpretation has to be carried out.

Discriminant analysis

Discriminant analysis belongs to the dependence analysis method, used to examine vectored and undirected effects between constructs. A prerequisite for such an effect analysis is the rigorous measurement of the theoretical constructs, which was already done for the constructs used in this work. The discriminant analysis measures effects between constructs whose direction is already determined. The use of this analysis requires data regarding the attribute variables of the elements (in this case, of the companies) as well as of their cluster affiliation. It is adequate for this work as the dependent variable; (that is, the companies' cluster affiliation has a nominal scale level) whereas the independent variables (that is, the single items developed for the description of the level of corporate globalization) have a metric level.[33] And it completes the cluster analysis already computed: the cluster analysis generates groups, the discriminant analysis examines *given* groups (Backhaus *et al.*, 2000, p. 147).

The analysis can answer the following questions (*ibid.*, p. 146):

- Do the single groups (clusters) differ significantly regarding the variables?
- Which variables are adequate/inadequate to differentiate between the groups (clusters)?

The discriminant analysis was computed in the following way: the companies' affiliations to the four different clusters generated through the cluster analysis formed the dependent variable, and all items developed for characterization of the level of corporate globalization were included as independent variables. In general, the procedure includes the following steps:

1 Definition of groups;
2 Formulation of the discriminant function;
3 Estimation of the discriminant function;
4 Examination of the discriminant function;

5   Examination of the attribute variables; and
6   Classification of new elements (*ibid.*, pp. 149ff.).

The first step was already completed through the cluster analysis as described above, that is, three groups were defined. The second step is to formulate the discriminant function, which should permit an exact separation between groups as well as an examination of the discriminant impact of the attribute variables. This function has the following general mathematical form (*ibid.*, p. 151):

$$Y = b_0 + b_1 X_1 + b_2 X_2 + \ldots b_j X_j \tag{3.2}$$

where Y = discriminant variable; X_j = attribute variable ($j = 1,2,\ldots, J$); b_j = discriminant coefficient for attribute variable j; and b_0 = constant element.

This discriminant function is also named the canonical discriminant function, and Y is the canonical variable and is at the metric level. Each group g can be described by its medial discriminant value, called 'centroid' (*ibid.*, p. 152):

$$Y_g = \frac{1}{I_g} \sum_{i=1}^{I_g} Y_{gi} \tag{3.3}$$

The third step, the estimation of the discriminant function, builds on the discriminant criterion shown in equation (3.3) above. However, this criterion must be improved by including the variance of the groups. The variance of the observed values (SS_y) is split up into an explained variance component (SS_b), (that is, the variance between the groups) and in an unexplained component (SS_w) (that is, the variance within groups) (*ibid.*, p. 156). The variable I_g indicates the number of observed values within a group. Thus:

$$SS_y = SS_b + SS_w = \sum_{g=1}^{G} \sum_{i=1}^{I_g} (\bar{Y}_{gi} - \bar{Y})^2 \tag{3.4}$$

Therefore, when analysing more than two groups, the following discriminant criterion can be used (*ibid.*, p. 155):

$$\Gamma = \frac{\text{variance between the groups}}{\text{variance within the groups}} \tag{3.5}$$

or:

$$\Gamma = \frac{\sum\limits_{g=1}^{G} I_g (\overline{Y}_g - \overline{Y})^2}{\sum\limits_{g=1}^{G} \sum\limits_{i=1}^{Ig} (Y_{gi} - \overline{Y}_g)} = \frac{SS_b}{SS_w} \tag{3.6}$$

The maximum value of the discriminant criterion

$$\gamma = \text{Max } \{\Gamma\} \tag{3.7}$$

is named the eigenvalue. The proportion of eigenvalue (= proportion of explained variance) acts as a measure for the relative importance of a discriminant function.

When maximizing the discriminant criterion, the ratio of the discriminant coefficients b_2/b_1 is determined. To get accurate parameter values of the discriminant function, it is necessary to perform standardization: the pooled within-groups variance of all discriminant values adds up to 1, and this can be calculated by dividing the variance of the groups through the degrees of freedom:

$$s^2 = \frac{SS_w}{I - G} \tag{3.8}$$

In this case, where there are three groups ($G=3$), two discriminant functions ($G-1$) at maximum can be determined, which are orthogonal to each other. This is valid, as the number of discriminant functions is smaller than the number of attribute variables (J) (*ibid.*, p. 168).

The next stage is the examination of the discriminant function, which demands the examination of the discriminant criterion. The common criterion used is Wilks' lambda,[34] which is an inverse criterion (that is, small values signify a higher release force) (equation (3.9) for the two groups case), because it measures the proportion of the unexplained variance to the overall variance (cf. Jensen, 2001, p. 105):

$$\Lambda = \frac{1}{1+\gamma} = \frac{\text{unexplained variance}}{\text{total variance}} \tag{3.9}$$

Wilks' lambda for more than two groups, assuming there are K discriminant functions, can be described in the following way:

$$\Lambda = \prod_{k=1}^{K} \frac{1}{1+\gamma_k} \tag{3.10}$$

where γ_k = eigenvalue of the kth discriminant function.

The examination of the attribute variables is important to explain the difference between the groups as well as to eliminate variables that are not of relevance. To be able to analyse the variables extensively, the discriminant coefficients for multivariate examination of the discriminant importance are taken.

The final stage includes the classification of new elements, and three different concepts can be distinguished: (1) the distance approach, (2) the probability approach, and (3) the classification functions. According to the distance approach, a new element i is integrated in the group g that is nearest to the element on the discriminant axis (Backhaus *et al.*, 2000, p. 180). This procedure is also the basis for the probability approach, which treats the classification as a statistical decision problem. The last approach was developed by R.A. Fisher (1936) and classifies the elements directly on the basis of their attribute values, but this approach can only be used if the researcher can assume the same variance in all groups (*ibid.*).

4
Empirical Study

Procedure of LoCG development

A mixed methods approach is suggested as the classical way for developing a measurement scale (Doney and Cannon, 1997, p. 43), because for a deep understanding of the research area both approaches, qualitative and quantitative, are needed. This view is supported by Kaplan (1964, p. 207) who states that 'Quantities are *of* qualities, and a measured quality *has* just the magnitude expressed in its measure.' Miles and Huberman (1994, pp. 40ff.) see the distinction between qualitative and quantitative as not well-aimed, rather preferring a differentiation between analytic approaches aimed at understanding few controlled variables, and systemic approaches aimed at understanding the interaction of variables in a complex environment. However named, the reader awakens to the fact that the combination of both approaches is appropriate for the reasearch question of this work: because on the one hand the linking enables the connection of the literature with issues important in management practice, and on the other hand it enables the elaboration of analysis providing richer detail as well as initiating new lines of thinking (cf. Rossman and Wilson, 1984, cited in Miles and Huberman, 1994, p. 41). The deductive and the inductive research approaches are combined because, for construct complexity reasons and for major differences and discordance in the literature, a purely deductive approach is not adequate (Homburg, 1995, p. 60). The methodological procedure chosen can be illustrated as in Figure 4.1.

Figure 4.1 Design linking qualitative and quantitative data

QUALITATIVE ⟶ **QUANTITATIVE**
(exploration)   (questionnaire)

Developing a primary understanding of the construct 'global' requires a qualitative methodology.[35] Narrative expert interviews are conducted within different industries[36] in order to examine variables constituting the level of corporate globalization from the point of view of commercial practice, and in order to compare these propositions with the literature (as discussed in Chapter 2). The qualitative research approach is chosen because corporate globalization is a complex phenomenon enabling different assignments of key characteristics. No single 'doctrine' exists. The hypothesis persists that theoretical approaches do not exactly meet reality in terms of the assumed degree of globalization as well as in terms of the use of global account management. This hypothesis is founded on a group discussion with 18 experts on key account management from different industries (chemicals, communications, beverages, and so on) in the context of SAMA's Best Practice Forum 2002.[37] Two main results can be stated from this discussion: companies scarcely differentiate between different forms of key account management (for example, international or global account management), and often pursue different forms in parallel. Furthermore, the national integration–national differentiation grid of Bartlett, and Bartlett and Ghoshal is often criticized (cf. discussion in Chapter 2) and the existence of transnational companies is questioned.

On this basis an interview guideline was developed including the following modules: key characteristics of corporate globalization, implemented key account management programmes (national, international or global account management and how these are defined) and key account selection criteria as well as procedure. The interviews are transcribed and put into the software NVivo® for analysis to link arising concepts and dimensions of corporate globalization. Of course, these interviews reflect the experts' subjective opinions, but it is useful to enhance the quality of the theoretically based development of indicators and to ensure the connection of theory with commercial practice and reality. Moreover, this procedure is the most commonly used in scale development practice (see for example Doney and Cannon, 1997, p. 43; or Homburg, 1995).

The result of the qualitative part is a preliminary model of indicators measuring the level of corporate globalization, with the characteristics constituting the basis for the item battery (that is, it is the instrument to measure the degree of globalization). These are combined with findings in the literature and reported back for refinement and development of indicators; the reporting back is used as an opportunity to enhance the 'validity'[38] of the qualitative research. The development of the measurement scale is based on the results of this qualitative analysis. This procedure enables the confirmation of the indicators measuring the LoCG that were defined *ex ante* on the basis of theory and empirical studies. The *definition of dimensions* is completed at the end of this stage.

The next step is the development of indicators; that is, the operationalization of the dimensions in the form of an item battery, which is packed in a questionnaire. Indicators are partly already developed in the defined dimensions of geographical and structural centralization versus decentralization, standardization versus national adaptation, global integration/coordination as well as resource allocation. The survey is conducted among a sample of exporting companies chosen from the Hoppenstedt® Database as well as the SAMA (Strategic Account Management Association) internet platform for members. The questionnaire design is aligned with the requirements of causal data analysis. Because the validation of the scale is conducted by a confirmatory factor analysis, the result is a confirmation or rejection of the indicators measuring the construct. In addition, the companies investigated must be categorized according to their different internationalization positions (that is, the classification of international, multinational, global and transnational companies).

If the chosen indicators actually measure the single dimensions, a cluster analysis is performed by using the factor scores of the identified factors measuring the LoCG. The cluster analysis enables the assignment of companies to specific types: probably international, multinational, global and transnational. Additionally, a discriminant analysis is undertaken to analyse which function separates best, which is the second-best, and so on, to determine the discriminatory power of the factors determining the typology's categories. In addition, it is important, as the construct LoCG seems to be of a complex nature,

Figure 4.2   Research design

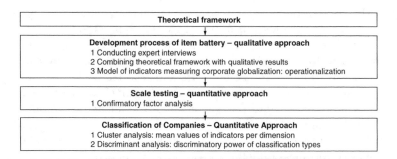

that the advantages of measuring a construct by several observed variables are taken into consideration (cf. Homburg, 1995, pp. 79f.). Figure 4.2 gives an overview of the research procedure.

Data collection and basis

The developed questionnaire was sent to a sample of 2,500 companies in Austria and Germany. The reason for this geographical sample restriction was to ensure comparability of companies (regarding cultural aspects and so on). Moreover, a company's administrative heritage is taken into consideration, defined as the configuration of assets and resources, historical distribution of tasks and responsibilities as well as ingrained organizational norms, values and structures (Bartlett, in Porter, 1986b, pp. 372ff.). The administrative heritage develops over time, and therefore an essential influencing factor is the date from when a company internationalized. This importance is underlined through the empirically demonstrated fact that MNCs in Europe and Japan developed completely differently. Historically, MNCs in Europe have predominantly shown a structure of decentralized, autonomous subsidiaries, but in Japan the centralized hub with tight control and limited flows of goods, information and resources from the hub to the subsidiaries is found. The date of beginning internationalization as well as historical growth definitely forms a company, and therefore companies were asked to indicate when they started to internationalize.

What remains then is the difference between organizations in different industries, and two possibilities exist to handle this problem. First, the empirical research could concentrate on one specific industry (for example, computer technology). This might be justified by the hypothesis of a company's LoCG dependency on the industry (supported for example by Kobrin, 1991, or Morrison and Roth, 1992). But the underlying hypothesis of our work is that each company can show an individual degree of globalization, with restricted dependency on the industry's position (supported for example by Ietto-Gillies, 1998; or Parvatiyar, 2001; Sullivan, 1994). Otherwise the measurement of a *corporate* degree of globalization would not be significant. The industry might of course be an influencing factor, but would never determine the whole degree of corporate globalization. Therefore, the second approach of choosing a sample across a variety of industries was chosen. The influence of the industry is of course taken into account when analysing the data and hypothesis testing will be done regarding this.

The companies were selected by the criteria of 'foreign activity'; that is, the companies have at least one foreign affiliate. Those companies pursuing at least some international activity in this way are comprised of both sellers and buyers. The sample was selected through the use of the Hoppenstedt® Database for Austria and Germany. Since in both regions the selection criteria 'foreign activity' brought up too many companies, the final companies were selected by systematic random sampling. First, a starting point t was randomly chosen from the first N/n elements of the main unit. Then, starting from this point t each $s = N/n - t$ element was selected. In this way 1,000 Austrian and 1,500 German companies were selected as the sample.[39]

The questionnaire was sent out on 4 July 2002 to all 2,500 companies, with a final date of return fixed for 31 July 2002 in the accompanying letter. The questionnaire is reproduced in Appendix 1.

Data analysis: qualitative

The data analysis results are presented in chronological order as described in the procedure and the single steps discussed above. The qualitative study was designed to explore the subject and to refine the items developed from the literature. The major question was, 'Are the indicators developed from the literature also relevant in practice.' Therefore, 13 expert interviews were conducted amongst global account managers (seller's point of view) from different industries and countries (Austria, Germany, Switzerland, UK). Global account managers were chosen as interviewees because of their intensive engagement and, therefore, expertise in the subject from the viewpoint of (1) global account selection (how to define what a *global* account is?) and (2) their own company's position (is their own company generally able to serve *globally*?). This was important for the major purpose of this work, that is, to derive GCM implications. The mixed viewpoint within the quantitative part of this work was chosen in order to test Bartlett's approach (our second research objective). The companies chosen are all intensively active in foreign markets and are rather big companies in terms of turnover and number of employees. The managers asked are in top management positions and have an appropriate overview of all organizational activities as well as of customer relationships. Moreover, all of them have international work experience. Therefore, these managers are considered as experts adequate for exploring the topic of this work.

The interviews had a duration of at least half an hour to two hours at maximum and were conducted mostly personally, but a few also via telephone and email conference (for reasons of accessibility and cost). In form and content, the interviews were divided into several parts: first, the respondents' orientations towards corporate globalization were scanned. Key characteristics of corporate globalization were requested twice: first, unaided recall was used to ascertain that all important issues coming to mind spontaneously were not confused or observed by immediately using a list of given items. Moreover, this procedure objectifies the researcher's previous, potentially subjective selection of items and is the classic methodological procedure in scale development (cf. Homburg, 1995, pp. 68ff.). Afterwards, the interviewees had to rank given items (developed out of the literature) characterizing corporate globalization according to their adequateness for describing corporate globalization (aided recall). The items mostly focused on issues regarding global strategy and processes. The final part was about global key account selection criteria, to find out whether or not the level of corporate globalization is of importance for companies working with global customer management.

The interviews were transcribed and exported as text files into the software program NVivo for analysis as follows. The transcribed interview texts are first coded in order to build categories of ideas, concepts, dimensions or items the interviewees are talking about. Within this process of coding, the program automatically places a finder to each category which enables the analysis of context and hypothesis testing. The 'places' where the categories are stored are named 'nodes', and can be divided into free and tree nodes. The researcher starts with coding into free nodes because at the beginning he knows nothing about the connections and dimensions of single ideas or concepts mentioned by the interviewees. The free nodes are coded directly out of the data. This technique is derived from the grounded theory approach where concepts 'come up from data' (cf. Bazeley and Richards, 2000; and Strauss and Corbin, 1998). During the coding process, the free nodes will – sooner or later – start to cluster around certain concepts/categories and are then led into tree nodes. Those tree nodes show some sort of hierarchichal structure (Figure 4.3) and already connect certain free nodes to show preliminary assumed relationships between items and dimensions.

However, hypotheses testing must be done in order to clearly define if there are relationships between single tree nodes. Testing might be done, for example, using intersection research for clarifying if there are intersecting issues between what interviewee 1 said with the found dimension 1 and the established item 2 shown in Figure 4.3. The tree nodes in this research represent the dimensions of corporate global-ization as well as the single items measuring them (see also the chart from NVivo in Appendix 2).

Figure 4.3   Example of possible tree structure in NVivo

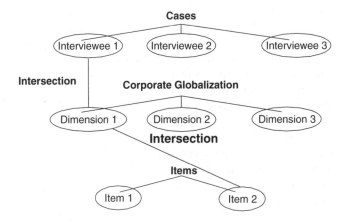

The tree structure developed for this research is listed below, where the numbers in parenthesis symbolize the hierarchy. For example, 'business mission' (1 1) means that the construct 'business mission' is the first subchild to node 1, which in this research is the 'respondents orientation of corporate globalization'.

- **Respondents' Orientation of Corporate Globalization** (1)
  - Business mission (1 1)
    Global vision (1 1 1)
      Geography bound (1 1 1 1)
  - Structures of power between HQ and subsidiaries (1 2)
    Central power influence by HQ (1 2 1)
      Geographical centralization (1 2 1 1)
      Structural centralization (1 2 1 2)
    Low influence of HQ (1 2 2)
      Geographical decentralization (1 2 2 1)

- **Corporate Global Strategy** (2)
  - Strategies for acting globally (2 1)
    Global branding (2 1 1)
    Standardization of products and processes (2 1 2)
    Global representation (2 1 3)
    Market entry mode choice (2 1 4)
  - High local adaptation (2 2)
    National product development (2 2 1)
    Product lines and plants (2 2 2)
    Portfolio of services (2 2 3)
  - The global player characteristic (2 3)
    Integration and adaptation (2 3 1)
      Global brand but national maintenance (2 3 1 1)
  - Coordination of activities (2 4)
    By virtual team structures (2 4 1)
    Specification of goals (2 4 2)
    Tracing of targeted goals (2 4 3)
    Coherent strategy and operation (2 4 4)
  - Cross nationality – geographics (2 5)
    Worldwide brand (2 5 1)
    Worldwide strategy (2 5 2)
    Worldwide staffing (2 5 3)

- Standardization by HQ (2 6)
  Finances (2 6 1)
  Products (2 6 2)
  Purchasing (2 6 3)
  Reporting (2 6 4)
  Sales (2 6 5)
    Globally standardized pricing agreements (2 6 5 1)
  Service (2 6 6)
  Preconditions of standardization (2 6 7)
  Processes (2 6 8)
  Core competence (2 6 9)
- Decentralization versus centralization (2 7)
  Decentralizing details (2 7 1)
  Centralized leadership (2 7 2)

- **Degree of Value-Chain Activities' Globalization** (3)
  - No globalization (3 1)
    Value-chain activities not globalized (3 1 1)
  - Single activities globalized (3 2)
    Globalized IT (3 2 1)
    Globalized marketing (3 2 2)
    Globalized production (3 2 3)
    Globalized purchasing (3 2 4)
    Globalized sales organization (3 2 5)
    Global communication (3 2 6)
    Standardization versus local adaptation (3 2 7)
    Globalized finance (3 2 8)
    Globalized controlling (3 2 9)
    Globalized process management (3 2 10)
  - Single activities locally adapted (3 3)
  - All activities globalized (3 4)

- **Corporate Globalization Drivers** (4)
  - Market saturation (4 1)
  - Technical infrastructure (4 2)
    Decreasing costs (4 2 1)
    Availability (4 2 2)
  - Culture (4 3)
    Own company's culture (4 3 1)
    Converging culture – Americanizing (4 3 2)

- Competitive issues (4 4)
- Coherence of strategy and operation (4 5)
- Human resources (4 6)
  Adequate quality (4 6 1)
  Adequate quantity (4 6 2)
- **Key Account Differentiation** (5)
  - No differentiation (5 1)
  - Global key account selection (5 2)
    Global key account selection criteria (5 2 1)
      Size of the company (5 2 1 1)
      Financial criteria (5 2 1 2)
        Total corporate revenue (5 2 1 2 1)
        Customer revenue with one's own company (5 2 1 2 2)
        Profit generation (5 2 1 2 3)
        Ratios (5 2 1 2 4)
        Potentials (5 2 1 2 5)
        Portfolios (5 2 1 2 6)
      Geographical position (5 2 1 3)
        Across country borders (5 2 1 3 1)
        Presence all around the world (5 2 1 3 2)
        Having a number of operating units (5 2 1 3 3)
        Number of foreign affiliates (5 2 1 3 4)
      Strategic fit (5 2 1 4)
      Value added (5 2 1 5)
      Relationship strength (5 2 1 6)
      Reference potential (5 2 1 7)
      Brand perception (5 2 1 8)
      Acceptance (5 2 1 9)
        One single strategy (5 2 1 9 1)
        No worldwide uniform pricing (5 2 1 9 2)
      Product fit (5 2 1 10)
      Commitment (5 2 1 11)
      Access to new segments or customers (5 2 1 12)
      Quality standards (5 2 1 13)
    Types of key accounts (5 2 2)
    Types of KAM programmes (5 2 3)
      Single form of KAM (5 2 3 1)
      Mixed KAM system (5 2 3 2)
  - Consequences of account differentiation (5 3)

- **Reasons for Using GAM** (6)
- **Global Processes** (7)
  - System requirements (7 1)
  - Share of knowledge (7 2)
  - Management commitment (7 3)
  - Converging of culture (7 4)
  - Information and communication flow (7 5)
- **Corporate Globalization Constraints** (8)
  - Product suitability (8 1)
  - Capital issues (8 2)
  - Restrictive company culture (8 3)
  - Risk estimation (8 4)
  - Legal and political constraints (8 5)
  - Industry (8 6)
  - Resources (8 7)
- **Respondents Personal Orientation of Globalization** (9)
  - Coordination (9 1)
  - Standardized products (9 2)
  - Geographic orientation (9 3)
    Financial criteria (9 3 1)
    Cross-national activity (9 3 2)
    Worldwide presentation (9 3 3)
  - Standardized sales (9 4)
  - Strategy (9 5)
    Standardized (9 5 1)
    Adapted (9 5 2)
  - Centralization (9 6)
    Brand strategy (9 6 1)
    Product design (9 6 2)
    Product sales (9 6 3)
  - Localization (9 7)

A graphical overview of this structure is given in Appendix 2, which also highlights intercorrelations between constructs and/or indicators. Very few intercorrelations could be detected with the intersection research used to test interdependence hypotheses. Before proceeding with the next step in scale development, the quantitative analysis, the single dimensions and indicators resulting from the expert interviews are described and discussed below. Within this analysis, the theoretically and empirically developed indicators are combined, which is the basis for the development of the questionnaire. The operationalization of the single indicators is summarized later in the chapter.

The first node builds the category *Respondents Orientation of Corporate Globalization*. This category consists of the company point of view described by the interviewees on what corporate globalization is. This point of view is often written down in a company's business mission, and is the reason why the managers were asked for their company's business mission during the interview. Some sort of global vision was frequently found (recognized as an important item for corporate globalization in the literature, for example Heenan and Perlmutter, 1979; see also our Chapter 2), incorporated in sentences such as 'we want to become the world leader in . . . ' or 'become the world's best . . . ' by the experts. However, global vision was mostly associated with geographic boundaries (country markets, and so on); the CEO of a major Austrian company stated for example, 'we want to be present in all European, Asian and American markets'). Moreover, the structure of power (discussed in the literature especially in connection with formal coordination mechanisms; for example Martinez and Jarillo, 1991) between the headquarters and its affiliates was of importance for a couple of managers. Interestingly, both extremes occurred: on the one hand geographical and structural centralization, attributed to the item 'Central power influence by the headquarters', and on the other hand geographical decentralization, expressed by the item 'Low influence of the headquarters'. What was not mentioned by the interviewees was structural decentralization. This fits into the theoretical framework since structural decentralization is one of the items strongly connected with multinational, not global companies.

The node *Corporate Global Strategy* includes not only strategies, which were described by interviewees, but also several other dimensions and items characterizing corporate globalization. 'Global branding', 'Standardization of products and processes' (named by the majority of experts stemming from different industries and pursuing foreign activity), 'Global representation' as well as 'Market entry mode choice' (cf. Dunning, 1977; Dunning and Pearce, 1981; Kotabe and Helsen, 2001; Nunnenkamp *et al.*, 1994; Wührer, 1995) were directly named as the items of the dimension *Global Strategy*. For this reason they were kept in a separate node – being aware of the fact that these items are not free of intersection with the other items submitted to the category *Corporate Global Strategy*, although this is taken into consideration for the survey construction. The other dimensions found are 'High local market adaptation', 'Integration and adaptation' in balance (expressed, for example, in terms of 'one integrated global brand, but nationally adapted maintenance of the brand', as it was formulated by the CEO of a major German company), 'Coordination of activities', 'Cross-nationality–geographics', 'Standardization' and 'Decentralization versus centralization paradigm', well known in the literature. High local adaptation is operationalized through the items 'national product development', nationally adapted 'product lines and plants' as well as through a nationally adapted 'portfolio of services'.

A supplementary category to global strategy is *Global Processes* which also contributes essentially to the level of corporate globalization. This node includes the following factors: 'System requirements', 'Share of knowledge, 'Management commitment', 'Converging of culture' (cf. Parker, 1998, or Tully, 1994) as well as 'Information and communication flow' (cf. Davidow and Malone, 1992; Knoke, 1996; Naisbitt, 1994). These factors are also operationalized and included in the measurement scale.

The node *Respondents' Personal Orientation of Globalization* includes all notions and aspects of the interviewees as experts dealing with the subject daily. The following factors clearly emerged: 'Coordination', 'Standardization of products and sales', 'Geographic orientation' (referring to financial criteria, cross-national activity and worldwide presentation), 'Standardized versus adapted strategy', 'Centralization' (of brand strategy, product design and product sales) as well as 'Localization'. Most factors directly relate to the factors named in the literature and discussed in the theoretical part of this work. What is noticeable is the fact that integration and interdependence were not mentioned by the interviewees when asked in the form of unaided recall, whereas both factors were considered as important in the aided recall section. Both factors will nevertheless be included in the measurement scale since, from the qualitative part, the conclusion cannot be drawn that integration and interdependence do not characterize corporate globalization nor that they are unimportant because of the conflicting results from unaided and aided recall. Interestingly, the interviewees still have a very strong geographically based understanding of corporate globalization (for example, for some

corporate globalization means 'being present in more than 10 countries' or 'doing business across borders', and so on), although in the
literature geography is assigned to internationalization. Since therefore
it seems still to play a major role for some companies, some measurement items focusing on this geography basis are included in the
questionnaire. This is also a good opportunity to compare whether
these geography-based items have a high discriminatory power as
opposed to the other items attached to the remaining factors.

The category *Degree of Value-Chain Activities' Globalization* includes
all interviewees' points of view on which value-chain activities
(purchasing, manufacturing, sales/distribution, marketing, finance and
accounting, human-resource management (HRM), and so on) are
globalized within their enterprises. The interviewees can be grouped
into two major clusters: cluster one comprises companies that have
already globalized all value-chain activities; cluster two has globalized
only *single* activities, where globalized IT, marketing, production,
puchasing, sales organization, communication, finance, controlling
and process management are named. Interestingly, human resource
management as well as R&D are not among those activities which
are globalized right from the beginning, but rather kept in the headquarters at this stage. It can probably be argued, with the help of theories found in the literature that range from the core competencies
hypothesis (Porter, 1986a,b) to the resource-based view (Penrose, 1959;
Prahalad and Hamel, 1990), that HRM and R&D are both counted
among a company's core competencies, and that they are valuable
resources whose application should be well deliberated. According to
the interviewees, the early globalization of these two activities seems
to be a question of the willingness to take risks. Cluster 1 also has
another quite interesting characteristic: although some activities are
globalized, single activities are locally adapted at the same time. Here
again appears a paradigm well known in the literature, that of standardization versus local adaptation. Standardization is one factor
associated with corporate globalization (see for example Levitt, 1983;
Montgomery and Yip, 2000; Morrison and Roth, 1992), whereas local
adaptation was originally linked to multinational companies (see our
earlier discussion in the theoretical part of this work). However, local
adaptation is definitely a factor of importance also for global companies – this relates to the findings in the literature that complex
global (transnational) companies balance between global integration

and local adaptation (Bartlett, 1986; Bartlett and Ghoshal, 1989; Ghoshal and Bartlett, 1998; Martinez and Jarillo, 1991). The difference between local adaptation in MNEs and local adaptation in complex global companies lies – according to the results of the expert interviews – in the fact that complex global companies adapt not necessarily nationally (that is, different products, strategies, processes and so on for each country), but regionally (that is, regions with internally homogenous, but externally heterogenous, needs and characteristics of customers are segmented and the adaptations are aligned with these differences).

What is noticeable is the fact that during analysis it came out clearly that some items mentioned were globalization drivers or constraints rather than determinants of the level of corporate globalization. As a consequence, these were filtered out and transferred into the two corresponding nodes *Corporate Gobalization Drivers* and *Corporate Globalization Constraints*. The factors representing drivers are 'Market saturation', 'Technical infrastructure' (decreasing costs and easy availability, especially, encourage corporate globalization), 'Culture' (one's own company's culture as well as the oft-cited trend of converging culture – sometimes titled 'Americanized convergence' by the experts asked as well as in the literature, see for example Fraedrich, Herndon and Ferrell, 1995; Parker, 1998; Tully, 1994), 'Competitive issues' ('We have to go global because our competitors did it' – a sentence often used for justification), 'Coherence of strategy and operation' as well as 'Human resources' (if available in adequate quality *and* quantity). Constraints lie especially in (1) 'Product suitability' (referring to the product characteristics, benefits, design and so on – are they suitable for the whole world or not), (2) 'Capital issues' (corporate globalization is associated with the need for a great amount of financial resources), (3) the 'Restrictive company culture', (4) 'Risk estimation' (the decision whether to take the risk to globalize or not is of course connected with the constraint 'Capital issues' described above), (5) 'Legal and political constraints', (6) the 'Industry' the company belongs to, as well as (7) 'Resources' (acting in parallel with the driver 'capital issues', because here corporate globalization is also associated with an amount of resources needed).

The last two nodes are *Reasons for Using GAM* and *Key Account Differentiation*. The reasons for using GAM arose from the question if and how global accounts were selected. This node contributes to the argumentation and supports the hypothesis that GCM is connected with the extent of corporate globalization and the demand ('pressure') for GCM from customers. This 'pressure' was specifically named during the interviews. The second node, *Key Account Differentiation*, is a category including several dimensions. First, two groups were distinguished – those pursuing no differentiation at all, and those pursuing global key account selection (the importance of the development of such a corporate globalization scale is also stressed by practice). For the latter, the selection criteria were specified as:

- Size of the company;
- Financial criteria: such as a certain total corporate revenue, customer revenue with one's own company, profit generation, or the companies' use-ratios, potentials and portfolios for the distinction of (1) global and (2) profitable and non-profitable customers;
- Geographical position: the global key customers must do business across country borders, must be present all around the world, have a number of foreign operating units or foreign affiliates;
- Strategic fit of both the customer and one's own company;
- The value that can be added for the customer and that is generated through the customer for one's own company;
- Relationship strength: loose relationships are likely to be of short duration, having no high long-term profitability and therefore holding a certain risk, which does not encourage long-term investments in the relationship;
- Reference potential of the customer;
- The customer's brand perception; and
- Acceptance: of one single strategy worldwide, the fact that no worldwide uniform pricing is available, product fit as a prerequisite, of the necessity of commitment on both supplier and customer sides, that new segments or customers must be reached and certain quality standards set.

The interviewees were then asked to specify which types of KAM programmes are used and which types of key accounts are differentiated. It turned out that both alternatives, using one single form of KAM or a mixed KAM system, occurred equally. Subject to this chosen KAM system, different types of key accounts were identified. GCM plays a major role for most companies and they try to select customers according to the criteria mentioned above, which for the firms define both whether (1) the customer is global or not, and (2) is profitable or not. But these selection criteria mentioned by the interviewees do not explicitly focus on the characteristic of corporate globalization (only the geographic approach), but are rather general criteria for selecting key accounts that are found in national key account management as well as in global customer management. Therefore, these criteria are only conditionally suitable for the purposes of this research and are, therefore, only used to a minor degree as scale items.

The node *Consequences of Account Differentiation* resulted from different annotations of the interviewees, but is not directly relevant for the development of the measurement scale.

Questionnaire design: indicator operationalization

The factors representing corporate globalization are operationalized in the following way. The first part of the questionnaire consists of anchor statements clarifying what the respondents mean by corporate globalization; these statements stem partially from the results of the expert interviews and partially from the literature described above:

1 Our company is integrated and coordinated worldwide in terms of decision making, programmes, implementation activities and resource application;
2 Our company balances worldwide integration and local adaptation in terms of decision making, programmes, implementation activities and resource applicatio;
3 Our company standardizes products, procedures, processes and technology as well as business strategies across countries with very minimal adaptations, if any;
4 Our company adapts to the national markets/countries where it is pursuing business/operating. (Definition developed from the literature, see Chapters 1–4, as well as by the interviewees.)

All items were rated on a seven-point Likert scale (1 = totally agree; 7 = totally disagree), which meets the requirements of the methodological approach used, the confirmatory factor analysis (LISREL).

The second part of the survey is characterized by the interrogation of purchasing decisions made in the single value-chain activities (cf. Porter, 1986a,b) by the use of oppositional pairs of attributes; that is, the geographically bound items as concentrated versus dispersed and standardized versus tailored are requested. In addition, the level of integration and coordination is inquired into:

A   Decisions in the following activities are performed completely concentrated (in corporate or regional headquarters) or decentralized (at local country levels)?

		Completely concentrated					Completely decentralized	
		1	2	3	4	5	6	7
1	Manufacturing/ Production	☐	☐	☐	☐	☐	☐	☐
2	Marketing	☐	☐	☐	☐	☐	☐	☐
3	Sales/Distribution	☐	☐	☐	☐	☐	☐	☐
4	Finance/ Accounting	☐	☐	☐	☐	☐	☐	☐
5	Research and Development	☐	☐	☐	☐	☐	☐	☐
6	Human Resource Management	☐	☐	☐	☐	☐	☐	☐

B   To what extent are programmes and processes in the following activities completely standardized across or completely adapted to each country?

		Completely standardized					Completely adapted	
		1	2	3	4	5	6	7
1	Manufacturing/ Production	☐	☐	☐	☐	☐	☐	☐
2	Marketing	☐	☐	☐	☐	☐	☐	☐
3	Sales/Distribution	☐	☐	☐	☐	☐	☐	☐
4	Finance/ Accounting	☐	☐	☐	☐	☐	☐	☐
5	Research and Development	☐	☐	☐	☐	☐	☐	☐
6	Human Resource Management	☐	☐	☐	☐	☐	☐	☐

C To what extent are the following activities globally integrated/
. coordinated or autonomous across countries?

	Completely integrated				*Completely autonomous*		
	1	2	3	4	5	6	7
1 Manufacturing/ Production	☐	☐	☐	☐	☐	☐	☐
2 Marketing	☐	☐	☐	☐	☐	☐	☐
3 Sales/Distribution	☐	☐	☐	☐	☐	☐	☐
4 Finance/ Accounting	☐	☐	☐	☐	☐	☐	☐
5 Research and Development	☐	☐	☐	☐	☐	☐	☐
6 Human Resource Management	☐	☐	☐	☐	☐	☐	☐

D To what extent does your company use resources cross-country to
support its business (i.e. resources from one country are used for
operations in another country)?

	Worldwide						*Local*
	1	2	3	4	5	6	7
1 Financial Resources	☐	☐	☐	☐	☐	☐	☐
2 Human Resources	☐	☐	☐	☐	☐	☐	☐
3 Equipments	☐	☐	☐	☐	☐	☐	☐

The third part measures the degree of corporate globalization according to the principles used in the literature to describe corporate globalization (again on a seven-point Likert scale). Of course, attention is
paid to what is described as 'representative' or 'non-representative'
characteristics of corporate globalization in Table 2.5. The hypothesis
is that (1) simple global companies should rate high on the interdependence, coordination and integration items, (2) complex global
companies (also called 'transnational' companies) rate high on the
latter *and* on the national differentiation items, (3) a high rate only

on the national differentiation level would be characteristic for MNEs, and (4) simple centralization and standardization is attributable more to internationalized companies (cf. suggestions from the literature discussed earlier in the theoretical framework of this work) than to global ones. Several mixtures of different scores on the mentioned dimensions will certainly occur, and it is the task of this research to group these mixtures to then show clearly the different degrees of globalization.

The items listed below are developed on the basis of the literature and/or empirical studies, with the sources named in parentheses. Some items came up only during the expert interviews and are identified as such. All items were scanned in the qualitative interviews, but only the relevant items are presented.

A Interdependence

'In my company competitive strategies in one country are significantly affected by our competitive strategies in another country.' (Leong and Tan, 1993)

'Knowledge developed in one country is widely shared across countries within our company.' (Leong and Tan, 1993; Expert Interviews; Mosquet, 2002, p. 224)

'Joint knowledge development projects are undertaken within our company involving cross-country resources.' (Expert Interviews, Discussions)

'Intangible assets such as brands, customer relationships, proprietary techniques are widely shared across countries.' (Leong and Tan, 1993; Expert Interviews)

'In our company assets and resources are dispersed and interdependent among international organizational units.' (Bartlett and Ghoshal, 1988, p. 66: provides a structural framework for the use of inter-unit cooperation)

'Our company employees have shared values and a common culture around the world.' (Martinez and Jarillo, 1991; Steger and Kummer, 2002, p. 193)

B Integration

'Overseas operations provide complementary contributions by national units to integrated worldwide operations.' (Leong and Tan, 1993)

'Global strategies are based on local inputs.' (Expert Interviews)

'Products are standardized wherever possible and localized wherever needed.' (Expert Interviews; Porter, 1993; and others)

'At various levels of our company, managers have international work experience.' (for example Parker, 1998)

'Our senior management has a world view of our business operations and opportunities.' (Bartlett and Ghoshal, 1988, pp. 71ff.; Heenan and Perlmutter, 1979)

'Our company has a significant number of brands that have similar images across countries.' (for example Parker, 1998; Porter, 1993, p. 141; Wilson *et al*, 2001; Expert Interviews)

'Our employees have access to required specific and general company information on a worldwide basis.' (Expert Interviews; Mosquet, 2002, p. 224; Von Müller, 2002, p. 677)

'Cross-functional and cross-national teams (both real and virtual) for specific projects exist in our company.' (Bartlett and Ghoshal, 1988, p. 70; Martinez and Jarillo, 1991; Mosquet, 2002, p. 225; Expert Interviews)

'Informal networks amongst people across countries within our company exist to support programme implementation.' (Martinez and Jarillo, 1991)

'There is frequent communication among national units to align each others' activities.' (Bartlett and Ghoshal, 1988, pp. 57f.)

'Local country units actively participate in the overall strategic planning and budgeting process of our company.' (Bartlett and Ghoshal, 1988, p. 70; Martinez and Jarillo, 1991; Expert Interviews)

'Our company has well-defined roles for individuals involved in national/international operations.' (Expert Interviews)

'National/regional/global goals within our company are clearly stated and aligned with each other.' (Expert Interviews)

'The company communicates a worldwide vision to both internal and external stakeholders.' (Parker, 1998; Expert Interviews)

C *National differentiation*

'Our company actively pursues any unique local country opportunities.' (Leong and Tan, 1993)

'Our company's products/services are fully adapted for each market.' (Leong and Tan, 1993; Expert Interviews; Mosquet, 2002, p. 224)

'Business strategies and programmes are uniquely developed for each country by our company.' (Leong and Tan, 1993)

'Assets and capabilities in each national market are considered unique to that country and rarely utilized for other country operations.' (Bartlett and Ghoshal, 1988, p. 64)

'Our company affiliates in individual countries rarely share the knowledge developed by them with other company affiliates.' (Leong and Tan, 1993)

D Standardization

'Our company's products are highly standardized across countries with very minimal adaptations, if any.' (Yip, 1992; Expert Interviews)

'Procedures, processes and technology applied across country locations within our company are highly standardized and minimal adaptations are permitted.' (Expert Interviews)

'Our business strategies across countries are very similar to each other.' (Leong and Tan, 1993)

'Our company's organizational structure in one country is a mirror image of the structure in another country.' (Leong and Tan, 1993)

'Application and knowledge in all countries within our company is undertaken in a highly similar manner.' (Leong and Tan, 1993)

'Our company's view about customer needs, wants and behavior across countries is the same.' (Parker, 1998; Expert Interviews).

'Programme implementation and the related decisions are coordinated across countries.' (Martinez and Jarillo, 1991; Expert Interviews)

'Rules and procedures in our company are standardized across countries wherever possible, and localized wherever needed.' (Martinez and Jarillo, 1991; Expert Interviews)

'Performance measurement metrics are similar across various national units in our company.' (Martinez and Jarillo, 1991)

'There are established processes for reporting programme progress and feedback from various national units.' (Martinez and Jarillo, 1991; Mosquet, 2002, p. 225)

'Our company adopts technology platform standards worldwide.' (Kearney, 2001; Kutschker and Schmid, 2002; and others.)

E Centralization–decentralization

'All significant decisions for regional and national operations are centralized within our company.' (Leong and Tan, 1993; Mosquet, 2002, p. 223)

'Individual country assets and resources are managed on a centralized basis within our company.' (Leong and Tan, 1993; Mosquet, 2002, p. 223)

'The procurement function within our company is centralized.' (Yip, 1992)

'Country managers have full authority in making procurement decisions for their entities.' (Leong and Tan, 1993)

'Marketing and sales functions are highly decentralized at the country management level.' (Leong and Tan, 1993)

'Country managers in our company have full profit and loss responsibilities related to all functions of the business.' 'Country managers make autonomous business decisions relative to their individual operations.' (Expert Interviews; Mosquet, 2002, p. 224)

'Country managers are required to generate their own resources for ongoing business operations within their country.' 'Minimal interference is exerted from headquarters for managing individual country operations.' 'Country managers often seek to adopt and leverage parent company resources and strategies.' (Leong and Tan, 1993; Expert Interviews)

'Country managers are free to cooperate or collaborate among themselves without seeking HQ approval.' 'The local governance of country subsidiaries is autonomous and HQ has limited influence on it, if any.' (Leong and Tan, 1993)

Following this part, a question is included referring to the interviewee's own estimation of their level of corporate globalization – presented on a scale from 'Not globalized at all' to 'Completely globalized'. This is intended for a comparison with the actual situation given by the results of the analysis and the companies' estimations.

The final part consists of demographic information as well as of geography-based information already used in empirical studies (see the discussion in Chapter 2 on measurement approaches) to measure the degree of corporate globalization. The demographic part contains questions on the respondent's position within the company, the industry, the number of foreign markets (on a country basis) in which the company pursues business, the starting year of foreign market activities, the main market entry mode chosen and the question if any form of key account management is pursued. The geography-based measurements include the ratio of foreign turnover to total turnover, the ratio of foreign employees to total employees, and the ratio of foreign affiliates to total affiliates.

This questionnaire formed the basis for the quantitative analysis and is shown in detail in Appendix 1.

Data analysis: quantitative

Descriptives

The effective sample consists of 276 questionnaires which were available until the end of August 2002 after following up activities. The return rate was therefore about 11 per cent.[40] About 60 per cent of the sample were Austrian companies, and about 40 per cent were German. The percentage of companies starting foreign activities before 1933 was 10.5, 12.1 per cent between 1933 and 1955, 25.1 per cent between 1956 and 1970, and about 52.2 per cent after 1970. As the date of the initial start of foreign activities was collected, it is included in analysis to test if there is any significant relation to variations in this date.

First, it is tested if the companies included in the return are representative for the basic inquiry population defined on the basis of the Hoppenstedt® Database. The attribute 'industry' is chosen for determining representativeness,[41] and Table 4.1 lists the effective industry distributions against those expected.[42] The effective distribution of industries within the sample is 11.3 per cent in the automobile industry, 19 per cent in chemicals, 11.3 per cent in food and beverages, 6.9 per cent in the computer and IT industry, 12.8 per cent in engineering, 6.2 per cent in textiles and 2.6 per cent in telecommunication, adding up to 70 per cent of the covered companies. The category 'Miscellaneous' has a relatively high percentage with 55 per cent, which can be explained mostly through multiple nominations. Many of the companies operate in several business fields: the main business could be applied to one of the given categories (for example, chemicals), whereas the other business fields were often too specific to build separate categories (especially in the technical areas).

Table 4.1 Comparison of effective and expected industry distributions

Industry	Effective industry distribution (%)	Expected industry distribution (%)
Automobile	11.30	2.40
Chemical industry	19.00	7.20
Food and beverages	11.30	5.04
Computer industry and IT	6.90	3.52
Engineering industry	12.80	13.60
Textile industry	6.20	3.60
Telecommunication	2.60	1.92
Miscellaneous	55.30	62.72

χ^2 adjustment test: $\chi^2 = 170.96$, $df = 7$, $p < 0.05$

The χ^2 test shows that there are significant differences: especially for automobiles, chemicals and food and beverages which are over-represented in the sample.

In evaluating the adequateness of the sample, it is important to question whether the right contact persons within the selected companies could be found. According to the complexity of the research area and the consequentially comprehensive questions, only the top management level was identified as being able to answer adequately. Figure 4.4 shows that 53 per cent of the contact persons were CEOs, about 20 per cent were sales managers or marketing executives and about 11 per cent were key account managers. Accumulated, 84 per cent of the contact persons were management executives and only 29 per cent had other functional positions,[43] thus affirming the answering competence of the sample and the representativity of this empirical work.

The distribution of the sample companies' turnovers is summarized in Figure 4.5, which shows that 29 per cent of the companies belong to the 'small' category with a turnover less than €10 m. There is also a large number (about 30 per cent) of companies which have turnover greater than €100 m. The H_0 hypothesis is that there is no difference between the two countries, and this hypothesis is accepted as the chi square homogeneity test shows $\chi^2 = 5.24$, $df = 5$ with $p > 0.05$; that is, no significant differences could be found according to the country (Table 4.2).

Figure 4.4   Distribution of contact persons

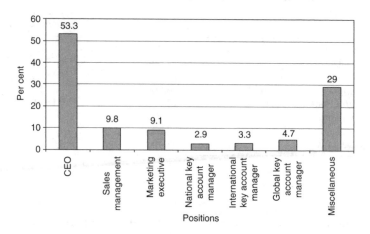

Figure 4.5   Total turnovers: a country comparison

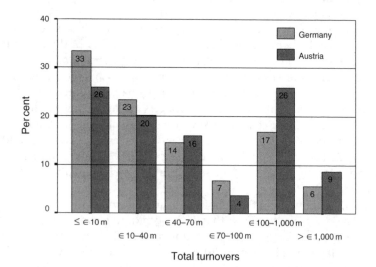

The relative turnover gained from *foreign activities*, that is, the percentage of foreign sales,[44] was surveyed. As Figure 4.6 and Table 4.3 show, the sample has a slight prevalence of companies gaining less than 20 per cent or more than 80 per cent of their turnovers from

Table 4.2   Cross tabulation: total turnover and country affiliation

Total turnover (millions)	Germany	Austria	Total
≤10	30	36	66
10–40	21	28	49
40–70	13	22	35
70–100	6	5	11
100–1,000	15	36	51
>1,000	5	12	17
Total	90	139	229

Homogeneity test: $\chi^2 = 5.24$, $df = 5$, $p = 0.388$

Figure 4.6   Percentage of foreign sales: a country comparison

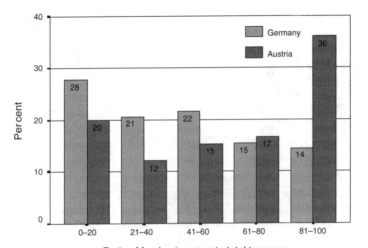

foreign activities. Also, a significant difference can be detected between countries as far more Austrian companies seem to gain over 80 per cent of their turnovers from foreign activities (in Table 4.3 the chi square homogeneity test $\chi^2 = 15.74$, $df = 4$, $p < 0.05$). This could reflect the fact that many Austrian companies have 'foreign activities' in Germany, as it is the most important market, very similar and close to Austria. Because the Austrian market is smaller than the German market, Austrian companies have developed foreign markets operations faster.

Table 4.3 Cross tabulation: ratio of foreign turnover to total turnover and country affiliation

Turnover (%)	Germany	Austria	Total
0–20	27	30	57
21–40	20	18	38
41–60	21	23	44
61–80	15	25	40
81–100	14	54	68
Total	97	150	247

Homogeneity test: $\chi^2 = 15,74$, $df = 4$, $p = 0.003$

Figure 4.7 Activities on foreign markets: a country comparison

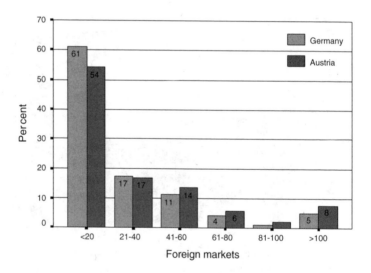

Another important descriptive variable is the number of foreign markets within which the sample companies pursue activities: 61 per cent of the German companies and 54 per cent of the Austrian companies pursue activities in up to 20 markets (Figure 4.7); whilst 5 per cent of German and 8 per cent of Austrian companies pursue activities in over 100 foreign markets. These latter could be referred to as 'global giants'. No significant difference could be found between Austrian and German companies (Table 4.4).

Table 4.4 Cross tabulation: number of foreign markets and country affiliation

Foreign markets	Germany	Austria	Total
<20	60	84	144
21–40	17	26	43
41–60	11	21	32
61–80	4	9	13
81–100	1	3	4
>100	5	12	17
Total	98	155	253

Homogeneity test: $\chi^2 = 2.08$, $df = 5$, $p = 0.838$

Table 4.5 Cross tabulation: number of foreign affiliates and corporate globalization

Number of foreign affiliates	Self-stated level of globalization		Total
	Low[a]	High[b]	
≤10	109	82	191
11–50	6	25	31
51–1,000	4	11	15
Total	119	118	237

Homogeneity test: $\chi^2 = 18.73$, $df = 2$, $p = 0.000$

[a]Low includes the scale levels 1 to 4 where 1 means not at all globalized. [b]High includes the scale levels 5 to 7, where 7 means totally globalized.

A cross-tabulation between the variable 'foreign affiliates' and self-estimations of companies' degrees of globalization (Table 4.5) was carried out in the next step. There is a significant tendency that highly globalized companies have a greater number of foreign affiliates on average. The same is true for the cross-tabulation of this variable with the statements containing the single characteristics assigned to different levels of corporate globalization. The tendency shows a connection in the sense that local adaptation is especially relevant for those companies operating with few foreign affiliates, whereas integration *and* adaptation seem more important, the more affiliates a company has (Table 4.6). However, no clear propositions can be made because 41.7 per cent of the cells have a frequency <5. According to

Table 4.6 Cross tabulation: number of foreign affiliates and statement regarding globalization

| Number of foreign affiliates | Companies' statements regarding globalization | | | | Total |
	Integration & cooperation	Integration & adaptation	Standardization	Local adaptation	
≤10	11	45	21	101	178
11–50	3	14	2	8	27
51–1000		9	1	3	13
Total	14	68	24	112	218

Homogeneity test: $\chi^2 = 19.55$, $df = 6$, $p = 0.003$

Bühl and Zöfel (2000, p. 240) or Field (2000, p. 64), not more than 20 per cent of the cells should have a frequency <5, otherwise the results can only be interpreted as tendencies. In both questions no significant differences regarding the country could be found.

The same distribution as described above within the variable 'number of foreign affiliates' was also found when analysing the number of foreign markets. Of course, there is a logical connection between markets and affiliates: many companies probably equate markets with affiliates, especially as they proceed further in their global development and build up over time more affiliates in those countries.

The data set shows that companies which started international business early (before 1933 or between 1934 and 1955) are more globalized than those which started after 1955. This suggests that corporate globalization is a development process needing time (Ohmae, 1990); that is, companies do not start business as 'global' companies. The basis of the χ^2 homogeneity test is the null hypothesis that there is no statistically significant coherence between a company's initial start of international business and its self-estimated degree of globalization. The result of the test rejects the null hypothesis and confirms a connection since $\chi^2 = 13.209$, $df = 3$ with $p < 0.05$ (see Table 4.7).

No significant difference could be detected between the variable 'start of business' and the country of origin ($\chi^2 = 7.628$, $df = 3$ with $p = 0.054$); that is, a very similar number of German and Austrian companies could be found within each of the three groups categorizing the start of the business. The same is true for a connection between

Table 4.7 Cross tabulation: how global the company is and start of business

Self-estimated level of globalization	Start of business				Total
	Before 1933	*1934–55*	*1956–70*	*After 1971*	
Low[a]	7	13	24	75	119
High[b]	19	17	38	52	126
Total	26	30	62	127	245

Homogeneity test: $\chi^2 = 13.209$, $df = 3$, $p = 0.004$

[a]Low includes the scale levels 1 to 4, where 1 means not at all globalized. [b]High includes the scale levels 5 to 7, where 7 means totally globalized.

companies' self-estimated levels of globalization with country of origin: again, no significant difference could be found (χ^2 homogeneity test: $\chi^2 = 2.13$, $df = 1$ with $p = 0.145$).

When analysing the connections between companies' statements on their major characteristics (1) integration and cooperation, (2) integration and adaptation, (3) standardization or (4) national adaptation, and the initial start of international business, a significant connection can be detected. When beginning international business (start of business between 1971 and 2002), companies mostly agree on national adaptation which is, according to the discussion in the theoretical part of this work, a sign of a low degree of globalization and a typical characteristic and a multinational strategy (see for example Ghoshal and Bartlett, 1998; Martinez and Jarillo, 1989; Porter, 1993). Those companies which started earlier (before 1933), and have more experience in working internationally, show a tendency to be globally integrated and nationally differentiated and cooperate among their units. This proposition is again based on the result of the χ^2 homogeneity test (Table 4.8: $\chi^2 = 19.652$, $df = 9$ with $p < 0.05$).

When correlating companies' statements with their vote on the scale of 'How global is your enterprise?', the hypothesis is significantly supported that 'integration and cooperation' as well as 'integration and adaptation' apply especially to highly globalized companies, whereas 'local adaptation' applies to less globalized companies ($\chi^2 = 53.16$, $df = 3$ with $p < 0.05$: Table 4.9).

No differences in companies' self-estimated levels of corporate globalization regarding industry could be found, with one exception:

Table 4.8   Cross tabulation: companies' statements regarding globalization and start of business (*a*)

Companies' statements	Start of business				Total
	Before 1933	*1934–55*	*1955–70*	*After 1971*	
Integration and cooperation	3	3	5	6	17
Integration and adaptation	13	11	22	26	72
Standardization	1	1	7	15	24
Local adaptation	7	12	23	71	113
Total	24	27	57	118	226

Homogeneity test: $\chi^2 = 19.652$, $df = 9$, $p = 0.020$

Table 4.9   Cross tabulation: companies' statements regarding globalization and companies' statements (*b*)

Self-stated level of globalization	Companies' statements regarding globalization				Total
	Integration and cooperation	*Integration and adaptation*	*Standardization*	*Local adaptation*	
Low	2	18	12	92	124
High	16	56	15	38	125
Total	18	74	27	130	249

Homogeneity test: $\chi^2 = 53.16$, $df = 3$, $p = 0.000$

telecommunications. All other χ^2 values had a significance level of $p > 0.05$ (Table 4.10). The fact that the telecommunications industry is significantly highly globalized may be due to the intensive merger and acquisition activities in this industry, where single companies have grown faster than average through these activities in worldwide markets. However, this industry influence is the only one found. Thus, this result criticizes all those studies that have built on the hypothesis that the industry generally influences the level of corporate global-ization, and that have developed measurement approaches on the industry level (for example Kobrin, 1991; Makhija, Kim and Williamson,

Table 4.10 Cross tabulation: industry and corporate globalization

Industry	Self-stated level of globalization		Total
	Low	High	
Automobiles $\chi^2 = 0.066$, $df = 1$, $p = 0.798$	16	15	31
Chemicals $\chi^2 = 0.279$, $df = 1$, $p = 0.597$	24	28	52
Food and beverages $\chi^2 = 0.407$, $df = 1$, $p = 0.523$	17	14	31
Computers and IT $\chi^2 = 0.089$, $df = 1$, $p = 0.766$	9	8	17
Engineering $\chi^2 = 2.573$, $df = 1$, $p = 0.109$	12	21	33
Textiles $\chi^2 = 1.732$, $df = 1$, $p = 0.188$	11	6	17
Telecommunications $\chi^2 = 6.976$, $df = 1$, $p = 0.008$	0	7	7
Miscellaneous $\chi^2 = 0.074$, $df = 1$, $p = 0.785$	75	75	150

1997; Morrison and Roth, 1992; see also theoretical part of this work in Chapter 2). This result therefore supports our decision to focus on the *company level*.

When analysing the cross-tabulation of the industry with companies' own statements described before, as well as when cross-tabulating industry with total turnover, all χ^2 values had $p > 0.05$, that is, no significant connection could be found.

Measurement dimensions of globalization

The aim in construct measurement is to assess the measurement instruments' suitability; that is, the goodness of the LoCG scale. As already described in Chapter 3 in our discussion of construct measurement, the goodness of such a scale is normally described by the concepts of validity, reliability and objectivity. To ensure validity and reliability, first-and second-generation criteria are used. Exploratory factor analysis belongs to the first-generation criteria, and has the aim of examining the assignment of the single indicators to the assumed constructs. The question to answer is which indicators load into which dimensions and how much of the variance they can explain. Cronbach's alpha and item-to-total correlations are also first-generation criteria used in this research. The general procedure and aim of a factor analysis has already been discussed in Chapter 3, and this chapter includes only the results of the analysis. The second-generation criteria are based on the confirmatory factor analysis and are examined in step two of this research. Both analyses, that is, the exploratory and confirmatory factor methods, together enable the validity and reliability of the measurement scale to be evaluated. Does the scale really measure the level of corporate globalization with the suggested indicators? This evaluation is presented with the help of the analysis results.

Before running the factor analysis, the database was cleared of missing values, to increase the quality of the results. This resulted in a revised sample size of $n=232$. However, there were still disturbances in the first stage of exploratory factor analysis due to a group of small Austrian companies which answered questions controversially.[45] This caused the problem that in the factor analysis method, no common 'system' of answers could be detected. The data from these companies caused dispersion in the data set as a whole which became unuseable. By using the single-linkage clustering approach, these companies could be identified[46] and were excluded, leading to an effective sample size of $n=130$ used for the analysis. This small sample size, of course, has consequences for the LISREL approach and acts as a limitation for the generalizability of the result (discussed in Chapter 5).

The first step was to conduct the exploratory factor analysis. The principal axis method was chosen together with the Oblimin rotation (set with $\delta=0$). The reason for this decision lies in the fact that the confirmatory factor analysis[47] acts on the assumption that factors correlate with each other. Therefore, it is useful to use a method that is also based on this assumption, the Oblimin rotation, for the exploratory factor analysis.

The scree plot can be used to determine the number of factors (see Figure 4.8). According to the apparent sharp bend in the plot's

Figure 4.8   The scree plot as determinant of the number of factors

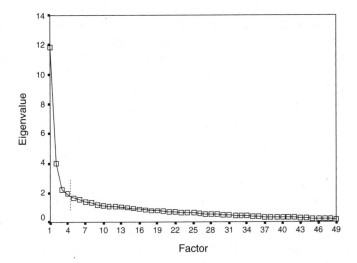

elbow curve, four factors can be determined. Kaiser's (1960), guideline that all factors with eigenvalues >1 should be retained, which is also often used to determine the number of factors, is considered as inappropriate for this data set because the number of variables is 49 in this work (the limit is set with 30 variables at maximum; cf. Field, 2000, p. 437) and the communalities (after extraction) of only 5 variables out of 49 are greater than 0.7.[48]

The other statistical requirements – tested to ensure the correct use of the factor analysis method – are summarized in the following results: the determinant of the R-matrix is > 0.00001 and no variables within the correlation matrix are highly correlated (the level of high correlation was set at $R > 0.7$[49]). The Kaiser–Meyer–Olkin test showed a level at 0.850 (recommended level > 0.5; cf. Field, 2000, p. 445f). Bartlett's test of sphericity[50] brought a result of $\chi^2 = 3{,}439.643$ on a significance level of $p = 0.000$, which would imply that the correlation matrix is *not* incidentally different from the identity matrix. In return, this would suggest that the output variables are intercorrelated. Bartlett's test is based on the assumption of a normal distribution, and, as already described, a normal distribution can be assumed for these data because the accredited limiting values in skewness of 2 and in kurtosis of 7 were not exceeded[51] (see West, Finch and Curran, 1995, p. 74).

In addition, other criteria are examined. The anti-image covariance matrix includes two parts of a variable's variance: the image and the anti-image, with the anti-image describing the part of the variance which is independent from the remaining variables. As the factor analysis is based on the assumption that the variables have common underlying factors, the consequence is that the variables are only adequate for this analysis if their anti-image is as small as possible. The general guideline is that the matrix is considered as adequate for factor analysis if the percentage of off-diagonal elements of the anti-image covariance matrix exceeding 0.09 is under 25 per cent (Backhaus *et al.*, 2000, p. 268). The percentage calculated from our data (about 1 per cent) is well below the named limits.

The major part of the residuals listed in the reproduced correlation matrix have values < 0.05 as recommended in the literature; 29 per cent of the residuals are > 0.05, which is acceptable according to the general recommendations (Field, 2000, pp. 446, 462). The general appropriateness of the entire correlation matrix is established.

The exploratory factor analysis pointed out the necessity of item elimination: 14 items out of 49 items remained. The loss of items was only partly due to cross loadings; most were eliminated because they had low factor loadings and were withdrawn in order to enhance the explained variance of the single factors to meet the criterion that at least 50 per cent of the variance must be explained by the items. Of course, the question is why only 14 items remained; developed out of the literature and from the expert interviews. Two explanations are conceivable.

First, those indicators suggested as important in the literature had in common one important factor: they were not tested and proved empirically. As already discussed in the theoretical part of this work, the research in this area has focused mostly on developing theories of global strategy and on the theoretical explanations of diverse phenomena in internationalization. Therefore, it is indeed interesting which indicators had no importance and did not clearly load onto one factor and were eliminated, and which were of importance.

Secondly, this research field is dominated by American researchers, which might imply that the indicators developed on the basis of this literature are only partly adequate for European enterprises since

German and Austrian companies probably show different globalization patterns and, therefore, place importance on different indicators or aspects to those of American companies. A follow-up study with an American company sample using this scale is recommended for further research (see the discussion in Chapter 5 on 'limitations and future research questions').

The 14 items that remain could be consolidated to four factors, which explain 56 per cent of the total variance (Table 4.12 below). This gives a first clue that there is discriminant validity. The four factors are listed in Table 4.11 with the relevant literature references to demarcate expected from new factors and to show the differences between the literature and empirical practice examined in this study.

'Standardization' is seen as a way to coordinate a company's single business and/or operational units. Therefore, some variables defined *ex ante* belonging to standardization or coordination in fact belonged to the same dimension. Coordination as a single dimension exists in this data set only in the form of personal coordination or rather interaction (cf. description below). This is new to the theoretical

Table 4.11 Empirically confirmed measurement dimensions and literature references

Factors	Name	Literature
F 1	**Standardization** to coordinate the enterprise units (6 indicators)	Levitt (1983) Bartlett and Ghoshal (1989) Ghoshal and Bartlett (1998) Morrison and Roth (1992) Montgomery and Yip (2000)
F 2	**Decentralization/localization** (3 indicators)	Leontiades (1985) Porter (1986a,b) Doz (1986) Bartlett (1986) Hamel and Prahalad (1985)
F 3	**Integration** (2 indicators)	Doz (1986) Porter (1986a,b) Prahalad and Doz (1987) Beamish *et al.* (2000) Kutschker and Schmid (2002) Wilson, Speare and Reese (2002)
F 4	**Personal interaction** (3 indicators)	New

considerations since 'coordination' has been said to be a single dimension (Martinez and Jarillo, 1991; Wilson, Speare and Reese, 2002), and a factor in the sense of 'personal interaction' has not been discussed before.

'Decentralization' or 'localization' is the second factor referring especially to the strategic level of business decisions (for example, local resource generation or local profit responsibility; see Bartlett, 1986; Doz, 1986; Leontiades, 1985; Porter, 1986a,b). 'Integration' was confirmed as a separate factor, that is as a separate principle determining the LoCG (cf. Kutschker and Schmid, 2002; Porter, 1986a,b, 1986; Prahalad and Doz, 1987; Wilson, Speare and Reese, 2002). The last factor, 'Personal interaction', partly contains items from the dimension 'personal coordination'. This factor shows very clearly that it emphasizes only coordination aspects building on personal require-ments such as personal interaction, as well as communication between people – that is, formal (teams and worldwide vision) or informal (networks; partly mentioned by Martinez and Jarillo, 1991, as important indicators, but related to 'coordination mechanisms') for successful globalization. Therefore, this factor was named 'personal interaction' and adds to existing theory as a *new factor* determining the degree of corporate globalization.

Most items and factors refer to the process and organizational level of the firm, only one factor to the personal level, that is, personal interaction. The items pointing at the importance of products for example, that is, product standardization (Levitt, 1983; Montgomery and Yip, 2000; Morrison and Roth, 1992) versus national product adaptation (Doz, 1986; Hamel and Prahalad, 1985; Porter, 1986a,b), had to be eliminated during exploratory factor analysis because they did not clearly load onto one of the four factors. The product level is therefore not an essential factor determining the LoCG.

The indications and factor loadings for each of the four factors are summarized in Table 4.12.

These indicators and factors were then analysed regarding their Cronbach's alpha: factor 1 had a Cronbach's $\alpha=0.858$. No indicator elimination to enhance the alpha was needed. Factor 2 shows $\alpha=0.753$; factor 3, $\alpha=0.732$; and factor 4, $\alpha=0.757$. The criterion item-to-total correlation was not needed for validity interpretation in this research, but the values of this criterion are also given in the summary tables below for overview purposes.

Table 4.12 Exploratory factor-analytical examination of the indicators

Factor (F)	Indicator[1]	Factor loadings[2] (after oblique-angled rotation)			
		F 1	F 2	F 3	F 4
1 Standardization to coordinate the enterprise units	Standardization of rules	**.599**	.009	.093	.130
	Similar knowledge application worldwide	**.562**	.067	.241	.017
	Similar performance measurement metrics	**.684**	.138	-.063	-.136
	Established reporting processes	**.658**	-.039	-.008	.205
	Coordinated programme implementation	**.633**	.071	.169	.053
	Standardization of processes	**.771**	-.113	-.053	.025
2 Decentralization/localization	Local resource generation	-.060	**.624**	.161	.098
	Profit responsibility of country managers	.124	**.693**	-.003	.038
	Autonomous business decisions	-.009	**.774**	-.057	-.052
3 Integration	International working experience	.170	.037	**.640**	.019
	Complementary overseas contribution	-.054	.002	**.826**	-.013
4 Personal interaction	Worldwide vision	.122	.217	.021	**.468**
	Cross-functional/-national teams	-.009	-.125	.059	**.902**
	Informal people networks	.120	.309	-.089	**.568**
Variance explained through factors		36.1%	7.9%	6.2%	5.8%

Notes [1] The original verbalization of the indicators is presented in the questionnaire in Appendix 1 (question 3). The questionnaire used for data collection was in German and has been translated into English for this book. [2] Indicates the amounts of the factor loadings. For each factor, the bold values show the same algebraic sign.

The four factors with 14 indicators were the basis for the next step in the empirical analysis: the confirmatory factor analysis, that is, the detailed examination of validity and reliability of the scale by the secondary generation criteria. The procedure of this method as well as the main differences between exploratory and confirmatory factor analysis have already been described in detail in Chapter 3. The tables that follow summarize all the results of the single factors' examination. They include, therefore, information also resulting from the exploratory factor analysis (item-to-total correlation, Cronbach's alpha and the explained variance). The secondary generation criteria for scale assessment were set in the way already described: 50 per cent of the global and 50 per cent of the detailed criteria have to be fulfilled for model and scale acceptance.

The indicator 'similar performance measurement metrics' was eliminated after executing the confirmatory factor analysis because the criterion 'indicator reliability' was not fulfilled with a value of 0.371. The indicator is therefore not included in Table 4.13. The other items meet this criterion. Regarding the other secondary generation criteria: $\chi^2/df = 1.98$, the root-mean-square error of approximation (RMSEA) is sharply on the limit with its value of 0.089, the goodness of fit index (GFI) is 0.970, the adjusted goodness of fit index (AGFI) is 0.909 and the comparative fit index (CFI) is 0.986. Analysing the detailed secondary generation criteria, the construct reliability is 0.829 and the average variance explained (AVE) is 0.529. Therefore, the 50 per cent limit set for this research is reached easily and factor 1 is accepted.

Considering the second factor 'Decentralization/localization' (Table 4.14), Cronbach's alpha is still at a high level of 0.753,[52] again suggesting that internal consistency of the measurement scale is maintained. Cronbach's alpha can suggest internal consistency, but not unidimensionality. The global secondary generation criteria could not be calculated for the reason shown below the table that three indicators have no degrees of freedom. What could be determined are the detailed secondary generation criteria: the indicator reliability, the construct reliability, and the average variance explained. According to these three measures, the second factor can be accepted.

A similar situation arises for factor 4 (Table 4.15), only Cronbachs' alpha ($\alpha = 0.757$) and the detailed secondary generation criteria were

Table 4.13   Factor 1: 'standardization to coordinate enterprise units'

1 Indicator information

Indicator	Item-to-total correlation	Indicator reliability	t-value of the factor loading
Standardization of rules	.660	.527	7.770
Similar knowledge application worldwide	.650	.595	8.226
Established reporting processes	.672	.504	7.602
Coordinated programme implementation	.701	.573	_[a]
Standardization of processes	.632	.450	7.184

2 Factor information

(a)	Cronbach's alpha	.858
(b)	Explained variance (exploratory factor analysis)	50.6%
(c)	Results of the confirmatory factor analysis:	
	χ^2 value/degrees of freedom	9.904/5
	(*p*-value)	(.078)
	RMSEA	.089
	P (RMSEA ≤ 0.05)	.177
	GFI	.970
	AGFI	.909
	CFI	.986
	Construct reliability	.829
	Average variance explained	.529

Note: [a] Value set to 1; therefore, no *t*-value is calculable.

calculated as this factor again contains only three indicators. On the basis of these measures, factor 4 is also accepted.

The third factor (Table 4.16) contains only two indicators, which makes it impossible to execute a confirmatory factor analysis. Therefore, only the first-generation criteria could be examined. Interestingly, the two indicators show a relatively high Cronbach's alpha with 0.732.[54] The item-to-total correlation is 0.579, and 57.8 per cent of the variance is explained by these two indicators.

After the determination and validation of these four factors, an exploratory retrograde calculation was carried out to determine

Table 4.14 Factor 2: 'decentralization/localization'

1 Indicator information

Indicator	Item-to-total correlation	Indicator reliability	t-value of the factor loading
Local resource generation	.551	.425	5.705
Profit responsibility of country managers	.612	.587	_[a]
Autonomous business decisions	.593	.519	5.799

2 Factor information

(a)	Cronbach's alpha	.753
(b)	Explained variance (exploratory factor analysis)	51.0%
(c)	Results of the confirmatory factor analysis:	
	χ^2 value/degrees of freedom	_[b]
	(*p*-value)	(–)[b]
	RMSEA	_[b]
	P (RMSEA ≤ 0.05)	_[b]
	GFI	_[b]
	AGFI	_[b]
	CFI	_[b]
	Construct reliability	.689
	Average variance explained	.510

Note: [a] Value set to 1; no *t*-value calculable. [b] This confirmatory factor model contains only three indicators and, therefore, has no degrees of freedom. For this reason, the calculation of the missing measures is not practicable.[53]

whether the indicators remaining from this procedure could be clearly assigned to the particular single factors. All indicators could be assigned back to only one factor in each case.

Afterwards, the next empirical step, a confirmatory factor analysis with all the 13 indicators remaining, was undertaken. The four-factor structure determined in the exploratory factor analysis is given here, and the results are presented in Table 4.17. The quotient χ^2/degrees of freedom is 1.79, the RMSEA is 0.068 and the CFI is 0.963. Only small deviations arise within the global criteria GFI and AGFI: at 0.899 and 0.844, both are slightly beneath the set limit. However, these deviations are very small, in fact negligible. Within the detailed secondary generation criteria, the indicator reliabilities and factor

Table 4.15 Factor 3: 'integration'

1 Indicator information

Indicator	Item-to-total correlation
International working experience	.579
Complementary overseas contribution	.579

2 Factor information
(a) Cronbach's alpha	.732
(b) Explained variance (exploratory factor analysis)	57.8%

Table 4.16 Factor 4: 'personal interaction'

1 Indicator information

Indicator	Item-to-total correlation	Indicator reliability	t-value of the factor loading
Worldwide vision	.544	.402	5.792
Cross-functional/-national teams	.618	.599	_[a]
Informal people networks	.609	.561	5.976

2 Factor information

(a) Cronbach's alpha	.757
(b) Explained variance (exploratory factor analysis)	52.1%
(c) Results of the confirmatory factor analysis:	
χ^2 value/degrees of freedom	_[b]
(*p*-value)	(–)[b]
RMSEA	_[b]
P (RMSEA ≤ 0.05)	_[b]
GFI	_[b]
AGFI	_[b]
CFI	_[b]
Construct reliability	.732
Average variance explained	.521

Notes: [a] Value set to 1; no *t*-value calculable. [b] This confirmatory factor model contains only three indicators and, therefore, has no degrees of freedom. For this reason, the calculation of the missing measures is not practicable.

Table 4.17 Results of the confirmatory factor analysis of the entire model

1 Single indicator information

Factor	Indicator	Indicator reliability	t-value of the factor loading	Factor	Indicator	Indicator reliability	t-value of the factor loading
Standardization	1	.529	8.094	Integration	1	.845	4.443
to coordinate the	2	.577	8.478		2	.396	–
enterprise units	3	.525	8.066				
	4	.587	–				
	5	.428	7.225				
Decentralization/	1	.446	6.381	Personal	1	.449	6.367
localization	2	.627	–	interaction	2	.482	–
	3	.455	6.421		3	.620	7.035

2 Factor information

Factor	Factor reliability	Average variance explained	Factor	Factor reliability	Average variance explained
Standardization to coordinate the enterprise units	.825	.505	Integration	.834	.517
Decentralization/ localization	.675	.510	Personal interaction	.769	.629

3 Complete model information

χ^2 value/degrees of freedom	105.567/59
(*p*-value)	(0.0002)
RMSEA	.068
P (RMSEA ≤ 0.05)	.128
GFI	.899
AGFI	.844
CFI	.963

reliabilities are all above the set limit as well as the factor loadings and the AVE being between 0.505 and 0.629.

The assessment of the discriminant validity – another detailed secondary generation criterion – can be performed by using the Fornell–Larcker criterion (Table 4.18). This criterion is chosen because

Table 4.18 Fornell–Larcker criterion

		Factor 1	Factor 2	Factor 3	Factor 4
	AVE[1]	0.505	0.510	0.517	0.629
Factor 1	0.505	1.000			
Factor 2	0.510	0.281	1.000		
Factor 3	0.517	0.275	0.107	1.000	
Factor 4	0.629	0.466	0.359	0.143	1.000

[1] AVE = average variance explained.

it is sharper than the χ^2 discrepancy test (Homburg, 1995, p. 85). As already discussed, discriminant validity is given if a construct's average variance explained is larger than each squared correlation of this construct with another construct.[55] Table 4.18 shows that this criterion is achieved.

Therefore, at least 50 per cent of the criteria are fulfilled. *The specified model is justified* and considered as *valid and reliable*. The scale measuring corporate globalization therefore consists of four dimensions with 13 Indicators.

The next step according to the aims of this research is the classification of companies according to their LoCGs; that is, by using the factor scores as classification variables. The adequate method for this purpose is cluster analysis. As the methodological foundations of cluster analysis have already been presented in Chapter 3, the focus here lies on the empirical results.

Cluster analysis

The aim of the cluster method used to classifiy the sample companies is to identify different levels of corporate globalization. The interesting question to answer is which factors especially characterize the different clusters? Is this comparable to literature suggestions or not?

The general process of a cluster analysis has already been described, and requires a decision on which classification method and algorithm to choose. Reviewing all advantages and disadvantages of the single methods, the two remaining possible methods for analysis were those of complete linkage and the Ward method. The Ward method can be considered as a good merging algorithm if (cf. Backhaus *et al.*, 2000, pp. 365f.):

1   the use of distance measurement is (textually) appropriate to similarity determination;
2   all variables are metric;
3   the data set contains no outliers;
4   the number of elements within each group is expected to be roughly equal; and
5   the groups have approximately the same extent.

Ward's method is inclined to build groups of about the same size and cannot detect sprawled groups or groups with a small number of elements. For the special situation of our work, Ward's method is inappropriate because it cannot be expected that the number of elements within each group is roughly equal or that the groups have approximately the same extent. From the objectives set for this research as well as from criteria used for the sample selection, a major difference is expected between the element numbers of the single groups: one could expect that there are few fully globalized (= transnational) companies (Leong and Tan, 1993) because the requirements in this category, for example simultaneous integration and national adaptation, are fairly high.

Therefore, the complete linkage method was used. This is especially appropriate as possible outliers were already eliminated with the help of the single linkage method before the first step, that is, the factor analysis, was carried out. This was done for the reason that the outliers also disturbed the result of the factor analysis.[56] As suggested by Backhaus *et al.* (2000, pp. 359, 367), the combined use of single linkage and complete linkage methods produces good and reliable results.

A three-cluster result could be detected by using the complete linkage method (with Minkowski metric[57]), after interpretation of the dendogram and the coefficients (Backhaus *et al.*, 2000). The classification matrix' coefficients show a clear leap from 4.301 to 4.907 between step 126 and 127 pleading for a three-cluster result.

The next empirical step is a test for significance of the result: how well can the single factors separate the clusters; that is, what is the discriminatory power of the single factors? Therefore, a discriminant analysis is carried out.

The companies' affiliations to the three different clusters generated through the cluster analysis was the dependent variable (*G*), and all four factors approved through the factor analysis were included as independent variables. All attribute variables were included simultaneously in the discriminant function. A univariate ANOVA as a complementary analysis was carried out to show how the single attribute values discriminate between the four groups (see Backhaus *et al.*, 2000, pp. 194f.). The *F*-test can be used to examine significance instead of the chi-square test. The result then corresponds to a simple analysis of variance (= ANOVA) between the grouping variable and the attribute variable (*ibid.*, p. 176). Table 4.19 summarizes the results. All variables show a significant level with $p < 0.05$; that is, the H_0 hypothesis that those variables do not discriminate must be abandoned and the H_1 hypothesis is accepted.

Two discriminant functions can be derived for three groups. Table 4.20 shows that the relative importance of the discriminant function 2 with 8.4 per cent eigenvalue (=proportion of variance) is much lower than for the first function showing 91.6 per cent. However, this is only a one-sided way of analysis, and to decide if the other discriminant function adds significantly to discriminate the groups it is necessary to examine the residual Wilks' lambda. According to

Table 4.19 Equality test of the groups' mean values with ANOVA

Attribute variables	Wilks' lambda	F-values	Df1	Df2	Sig.
Factor 1: standardization	.462	74.039	2	127	.000
Factor 2: localization/ decentralization	.536	54.986	2	127	.000
Factor 3: Integration	.676	30.419	2	127	.000
Factor 4: Personal interaction	.406	92.881	2	127	.000

Table 4.20 Eigenvalues (factor scores used)

Function	Eigenvalue	% of variance	Accumulated %	Canonical correlation
1	4.091	91.6	91.6	.896
2	.376	8.4	100.0	.523

Table 4.21   Wilks' lambda (factor scores used)

Test of functions	Wilks' lambda	Chi square	df	Sig.
1 to 2	.143	244.301	8	.000
2	.727	40.064	3	.000

Table 4.22   Mean discriminant coefficient for the four factors

Attribute values	Function		Mean discriminant coefficient
	1	2	
Factor 1: standardization	.534	.087	.496
Factor 2: localization/ decentralization	.578	.660	.584
Factor 3: integration	.507	.286	.488
Factor 4: personal interaction	.536	−.773	.556

Table 4.21, the second discriminant function also adds significantly to the discrimination of the groups. Therefore, both functions together significantly discriminate among the three groups.

The standardized discriminant coefficients reflect the importance of the attribute variables within the two discriminant functions. Regarding the four factors, factor 2 'localization/decentralization' has the highest discriminant importance for function 1, and factor 4, 'personal interaction', for function 2. But to examine the discriminant importance of an attribute variable regarding *all* discriminant functions, the absolute coefficients' values have to be weighted with the proportion of eigenvalue of the anent discriminant function to calculate the middle discriminant coefficients. A summary of those coefficients for the factors is presented in Table 4.22.

When interpreting the mean discriminant coefficients for the four factors, it becomes clear that factor 2 'localization/decentralization' discriminates best, followed by factor 4 'personal interaction'.

The structure matrix is shown in Table 4.23 for the four factors. Variables with large coefficients for a particular function are grouped together to facilitate interpretation, and the values are marked with asterisks to show for which function they are largest.

Table 4.23 Structure matrix for the four factors

Attribute values	Function	
	1	*2*
Factor 1: standardization	.534*	−.029
Factor 3: integration	.335*	.223
Factor 4: personal interaction	.552	−.758*
Factor 2: localization/decentralization	.431	.534*

Table 4.24 Results of classification according to the factors

Complete linkage			Predicted group membership			Total
			1	*2*	*3*	
Original group membership	Number	1	56	6	0.0	62
		2	9	46	0.0	55
		3	0	0	13	13
	%	1	90.3	9.7	0.0	100.0
		2	16.4	83.6	0.0	100.0
		3	.0	.0	100.0	100.0

Of the originally grouped cases 88.5 per cent were classified correctly. All 130 cases were used.

The classification statistics for this discriminant analysis according to the factors is presented in Table 4.24. Within the factors, the hit rate is 88.5 per cent. But as the three groups are of different size, one has to weight the classification hit ratio statistically. Given the three groups, assessed according to their different size, a hit ratio of 90.3 per cent for group 1, 83.6 per cent for group 2 and 100.0 per cent for group 3 is reached. Compared to a classification by chance alone, one would expect a hit ratio of 47.7 per cent for group 1, 42.3 per cent for group 2 and 10 per cent for group 3. Therefore, the improvement over chance is about 42.6 per cent for group 1, 41.3 per cent for group 2 and even 90 per cent for group 3, resulting in an average improvement of about 58 per cent (arithmetic mean over all groups). This indicates satisfactory validity. The scatter plot is illustrated in Figure 4.9.

Figure 4.9   The canonical discriminant function presented as a scatter plot

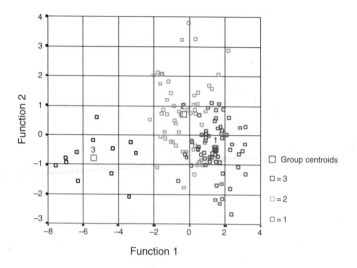

Function 1

A second relevant presentation of the classification is a territorial map (Figure 4.10). Such a map shows the areas (territories), which mark a group's affiliation field. The classification probability is higher within the borders of the territories for a particular group than for the other groups. On the border lines, the classification probability is the same for the bordering goups, which correspond to the critical discriminant value on the discriminant axis (Backhaus *et al.*, 2000, pp. 203f.).

Cluster characterization

The single clusters detected can be characterized verbally according to the indicators that separate the groups best. As companies decide to globalize, they start to develop capabilities which are characteristic for each degree of globalization. Each 'higher' degree includes all capabilities developed first *and* the new capability(ies) needed for the next level (phenomenon of dynamics in development). This can be explained through the fact that knowledge learnt once to fulfil a goal is not forgotten when striving for other objectives; rather, companies pursue knowledge management during their development. Therefore, the three groups of clusters probably reach from a very low to

Figure 4.10 Territorial Map

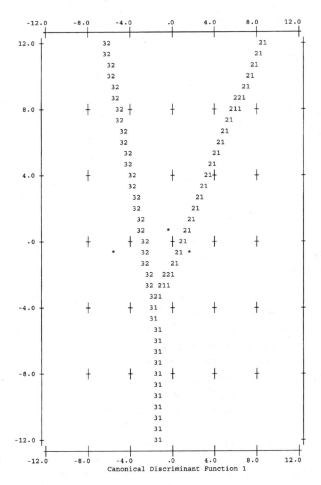

Canonical Discriminant Function 1

a high degree of globalization. This developmental view of corporate globalization is also noted in the literature (Ohmae, 1990).

Cluster 3 can be characterized as the cluster of 'beginners' and includes 13 companies. These companies show low values in general, probably still operate at a rather national level and have just begun to develop towards globalization; they show a certain level of standardization and integration (Table 4.25). This group corresponds best to what the literature often denominates as an 'international company'

Table 4.25   Factor means comparison regarding the three groups – based on ANOVA

Factor	Clusters	Mean[a]	Significance
Standardization	1	5.17	.000
	2	4.30	
	3	2.00	
Localization decentralised	1	5.30	.000
	2	5.24	
	3	1.80	
Integration	1	5.31	.000
	2	4.90	
	3	2.54	
Personal interaction	1	5.60	.000
	2	3.66	
	3	1.90	

[a] 'Mean' designates the arithmetic mean of the indicators within a factor, based on the single groups.

with regiocentric orientation (see Bartlett and Ghoshal, 1989; Heenan and Perlmutter, 1979; Sera, 1992). However, the difference is that cluster 3 companies have very few affiliates, if any. These companies are really at the beginning and are therefore named 'beginners' instead of 'internationals' in this work to underline this fact.

The factor 'localization/decentralization' dominates cluster 2 with 55 members. However, this cluster also shows a certain capability to standardize. The parameter values of the factor 'integration' are rather high, which could be explained through the fact that high localization and, in parallel, a certain standardization can only be fulfilled through integration of activities and processes. Cluster 2 corresponds exactly to what is called a multinational company (see for example Beamish *et al.*, 2000; Ghoshal and Bartlett, 1998; Heenan and Perlmutter, 1979). The local business units make autonomous decisions and are expected to generate their own resources[58] and bear responsibility; that is, the local units are seen as independent units only influenced by the headquarters to a certain extent to sustain and ensure that the topmost directives and aims are achieved. Cluster 2 mostly corresponds to theoretical considerations found in international management, strategy and marketing literature and discussed in the theoretical part of this work. Factor 4 'personal interaction' shows low parameter values in this cluster.

Cluster 1 includes the fully globalized companies ($n = 62$) that are characterized by high values on all factors. The special focus of this cluster is on the factor 'personal interaction'; this factor is *the* unique attribute of cluster 1 companies. Moreover, this cluster incorporates two opposite factors: localization/decentralization and integration. Therefore, the characteristic of this cluster equates to the description of 'transnational' companies in the literature (Bartlett, 1986). The question has always remained as to whether such transnational companies exist or not, but the empirical data in this research supports the thesis that such enterprises really operate in the world.

What could not be found is a cluster of companies meeting the criteria defined by Ghoshal and Bartlett (1998) and Bartlett (1986) for '[simple] global' companies. Only the 'transnational' category could be proven showing the highest degree of globalization.

Cluster demographics

The clusters can be characterized by demographics of the companies (Table 4.26), but one can only discuss *tendencies* because often the numbers of the single cells are below 5 which is relevant for chi-squared homogeneity tests by cross-tabulations (cf. Field, 2000, pp. 64 and 66). There is no difference according to the industry to which the companies in the single clusters belong (confirming the fact that the LoCG is independent of industry, which was also valid for the whole data set in general). The percentage of turnover gained from foreign activities is higher in clusters 1 and 2 than in 3, and the same is true for the number of foreign markets operated in. Regarding total turnover, it is seen that firms with a high turnover belong to cluster 1 or 2, that is, are more globalized than smaller enterprises. Those companies just starting their international business have a total turnover below €40 m, those already experiencing global business have a turnover greater than €40 m, and a significant number of them feature more than €100 m. The number of employees also varies according to the cluster: clusters 1 and 2 include huge companies having more than 1,000 employees, whereas cluster 3 includes rather small companies with numbers of employees between 50 and 500 (that is, typical SMEs[59]).

Table 4.26   Cluster demographics of the three groups – based on ANOVA

Variables	Clusters	N	Mean	Significance
Percentage of foreign sales to total	1	62	59.5	.021
sales 2001	2	55	59.2	
	3	13	25.6	
Total turnover 2001 (millions)	1	62	3,587	.127
	2	55	1,104	
	3	13	20	
Number of employees	1	62	35,306	.011
	2	55	4,890	
	3	13	158	
Number of different employees' nationalities	1	62	38	.020
	2	55	22	
	3	13	2	
Number of foreign affiliates	1	62	35	.011
	2	55	13	
	3	13	1	
Start of international activities	1	62	1922	.470
	2	55	1962	
	3	13	1974	
Number of foreign markets	1	62	61	.002
	2	55	38	
	3	13	1	

Analysing the number of foreign affiliates, cluster 1 companies have the highest number of foreign affiliates, followed by cluster 2 (the multinational companies). Cluster 3 has – if any – up to 10 affiliates maximum. This corresponds to the proposition from the literature that to enhance national differentiation (Doz, 1986; Hamel and Prahalad, 1985; Porter, 1986a,b), a certain number of affiliates is required. The extreme case in this category would be to have an affiliate in each country a company operates in. Cluster 3 has just started the 'international career' and first tries to standardize processes and systems to be able to coordinate international business (cf. Bartlett and Ghoshal, 1989; Hordes, Clancy and Baddaley, 1995; Levitt, 1983; Sera, 1992). This also corresponds to the GCM approach of Wilson *et al.* (2002) that differentiates between different GCM development stages (see also p. 46 ff. of this work): the first stage, the early GCM, tends to be centralized and standardized and could be adequately used by and for companies belonging to cluster 3.

Our results also clearly show that standardization plays a major role in the international business life of German or Austrian companies. This was already indicated in the qualitative part of our analysis as well as in the literature (cf. Levitt, 1983; or Montgomery and Yip, 2000; Morrison and Roth, 1992), and was expected for this data set. The standardization is enhanced by having only those affiliates that are absolutely needed (for example, for sales and distribution; these value-chain activities have to be globalized first, are still supervised by headquarters at the beginning and are later on decentralized, cf. Ohmae, 1990). The more separate units exist, the more effort is needed to capture all in a standardized system.

Regarding the statement about companies' main orientation, the cluster 2 companies mainly named 'localization' as their guiding principle, whereas cluster 1 companies named 'integration', 'coordination' and 'localization' as important factors. This corresponds to the fact that cluster 2 is the 'multinational' cluster, characterized by a high value of the factor 'localization/decentralization'. Cluster 1 companies are the fully globalized ones; as they reach integration, coordination and localization, they fulfill the premises of companies called 'transnational' (Bartlett, 1986) or 'global players' (Parvatiyar and Gruen, 2001) in the literature. Cluster 3 represents what Parvatiyar and Gruen (2001) have called 'global aspirants' in their GCM theory (see also the discussion in Chapter 2) – companies that show a low level of worldwide integration as well as localization.

Globalization can be a development companies pass through, beginning at a low degree, then becoming multinational and at last fully globalized. Each cluster shows a distinct concentration on different factors, but the developmental orientation is supported by the fact that from the 'beginners' (cluster 3) up to the 'globals' (cluster 1) each cluster shows partly the same values of factors that were important in the cluster before (that is, cluster 2 has the characteristics of cluster 3 *and* its own main focus; cluster 1 has the characteristics of cluster 2 and 3 *and* its own focus). The factors that are taken along from other clusters show values that are almost equal to the ones from the cluster which concentrates on those. The factor's own cluster's focus values are of course highest.

If globalization is considered as an evolutionary development, it includes a time factor. Therefore, the starting point of international business would be expected to correlate positively with the degree of corporate globalization (see our earlier considerations in the theoretical part of this work, as well as the cross-tabulation result of companies' own estimations of their LoCG with their start of business, where a significant connection was found). However, this correlation cannot be proved when using the three-cluster result grouping companies according to their LoCG and, therefore, presents a conflicting result. Companies of different age are also not significantly spread in the three groups according to their origin (Germany or Austria).

A feasible explanation for the first phenomenon above could be the fact that only the companies themselves determine whether they pass through these stages or if they remain in one category. It is rather a strategic decision influenced by many different internal and external factors. There is no need or force to fully globalize – in contrast to considerations in the literature that only global companies will survive the intensive, worldwide competition in future (cf. Ohmae, 1990). This is supported by the fact that the kind of industry companies operate in does not correlate positively with the degree of corporate globalization (with the exception of the telecommunications industry), that is, with one of the three clusters.

Therefore, the globalization process described above is the *typical way* companies take *if* they want to develop their worldwide business further.

Comparison to the existing measurement literature

The results of this empirical study add to the existing literature on GCM. Senn and Zeier's (2002) model (discussed in Chapter 2, pp. 49 f.) presents nine key enablers of the key account management process that can be set in connection with the variables resulting from this research: the development process of key account management is based on the same dimensions as corporate globalization, namely on organizational process and system changes as well as on the staff (called 'people' in Senn and Zeier's model and specified as factor 'personal interaction' in this work). Senn and Zeier's model was criticized as too little differentiated in the theoretical part of this work to be able to give actional instructions whose variables might help, for example, to align organizational structures and processes. In our work, the single dimensions and factors are specified and put in concrete form to be able to derive strategic and tactical implications (for example, the constitution of cross-national and cross-functional teams to leverage corporate globalization which was discussed in detail before). A detailed discussion of theoretical and managerial implications is presented in Chapter 5.

So far, most variables named in the literature characterizing international, multinational or global firms, that is, aimed to conceptualize these constructs, have been barely examined empirically. Therefore, our empirical study also adds to the existing measurement approaches. A comparison of existing approaches and our scale is discussed below.

Only the study of Martinez and Jarillo (1991) and that of Leong and Tan (1993) have tried empirically to prove theoretical considerations: Martinez and Jarillo examined the dimension 'coordination' whereas Leong and Tan tried to confirm Bartlett and Ghoshal's national integration–national differentiation grid (which could be confirmed only partly; the proof of the existence of transnational companies, for example, could not be adduced). The other studies already discussed before in this work include mainly geographically-based measures (cf. Gestrin, Knight and Rugman, 1999a; Ietto-Gillies, 1998; Ruigrok and Wagner, 2000; UNCTAD, 1998; Van Tulder and Ruigrok, 1996; and van den Berghe, 2001), focus on the industry level instead of the corporate level (for example Kobrin, 1991; Makhija, Kim and Williamson, 1997) or are index-based (for example Sullivan's DOI, 1994; the disadvantages of indices were already discussed in the theoretical part of this work). Therefore, our research adds not only to the existing knowledge of the concept of corporate globalization, but examines which indicators really measure the concept and which do not, based on a European data set of companies.

Regarding the existing measurement approaches discussed in the theoretical part of this work, the only *dimension* stated in literature which could be proved in this study is standardization. However, the single approaches focused especially on product standardization (cf. Montgomery and Yip, 2000 and Morrison and Roth, 1992) whereas this study has shown that only structural and process standardization are of major relevance in determining the LoCG. The factor 'personal interaction' is only taken into account by Kearney (2001) as the dimension 'personal contact'. However, Kearney operationalized this dimension on the national level; therefore, the single indicators are completely different. The other two factors did not feature in any of the other empirical studies. However, one single indicator that also turned out to be important in this research could be isolated from the other studies: top managers' international work experience was already examined by Sullivan (1994) and included in his 'attitudinal attributes' as well as in the further development by van den Berghe (2001) in the category 'orientation'.

The RDI approach (Research and Development intensity Indicator, measuring the share of R&D activities abroad; cf. Cantwell, 1989 and van den Berghe, 2001) is also not adequate for measuring the LoCG according to this research because no significant difference between groups with different LoCG's regarding R&D activities could be found. In consequence, the RDI cannot determine different levels of corporate globalization.

The other two factors, integration and localization, were not operationalized explicitly in any of the discussed measurement approaches, and were only mentioned by Montgomery and Yip (2000) as important factors.

Those measurement approaches focusing on ratios such as the ratio of foreign sales to total sales (cf. Sullivan, 1994; UNCTAD, 1998; van Tulder and van den Berghe, 1998) are only conditionally suitable for measuring the LoCG: companies showing a high LoCG also show a high percentage of foreign turnover/sales, but these measurement approaches, for example, could not differentiate between cluster 1 and cluster 2 companies because both of them have a high percentage. Therefore, these approaches may be adequate for a fast and simple estimation of a company's LoCG, but neither for a detailed segmentation approach as needed for GCM nor as a basis for conscious strategic corporate planning.

Excursion

The theoretical state-of-the-art 'scheme' of globalization – the national integration/national differentiation grid of Bartlett (1986), Bartlett and Ghoshal (1989) and Ghoshal and Bartlett (1998) – is criticized because there has been no empirical proof so far that the matrix maps reality. The design of our own research enables a comparison of the theoretical approach with practice, but this can only be done if one uses a two-dimensional approach for making the clusters and differences between them visible. The general cluster analysis carried out before was

Figure 4.11   Companies clustered by factor 2 and factor 3

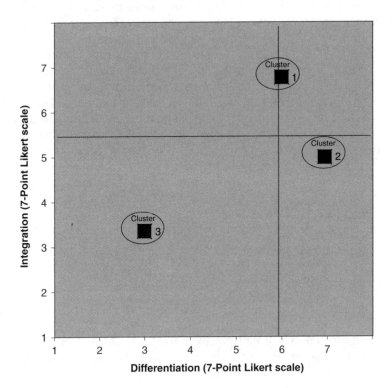

conducted on a multi-dimensional (all four factors included as classification variables) level and cannot be presented graphically. Therefore, the companies within this sample are clustered again using only factors 2 and 3.

Factor 2 is the localization/decentralization dimension and factor 3 the integration dimension. It was tested how the companies clustered according to these two factors and, afterwards, how they differ between the groups according to factors 1 and 4; that is, to standardization and personal interaction. The results of the two-dimensional analysis are presented in Figure 4.11. Factors 2 and 3, differentiation and integration, are chosen because they correspond to the dimensions used in Bartlett and Ghoshal's grid.

When using only factors 2 and 3 as clustering variables, three groups of companies can be distinguished in Figure 4.11 and not four as suggested by Bartlett and Ghoshal. The squares represent the cluster centres, built through the mean value of each group within the two dimensions of integration and differentiation. Cluster 1 shows high values on both dimensions, that is, companies belonging to this group are highly integrated and localized at the same time (the mean value of all variables measuring integration is 5.80, the mean of all localization variables is 4.94). Cluster 2 companies are far more localized than integrated (mean value of localization variables is 6.0 whereas the mean of integration variables is 3.99). The first two clusters are comparable to clusters 1 and 2 in the cluster analysis done before, where all four factors were included for classification purposes. Therefore, cluster 1 can again be called the transnational/global cluster and cluster 2 the multinational cluster. Cluster 3 shows low values on both dimensions, that is, the mean value of integration variables is about 2.35 and the mean value of localization variables is exactly 2.0. This could represent the companies that have just started to globalize, the 'internationals' in Bartlett and Ghoshals's typology, but named 'beginners' before in this work.

Regarding factors 1 and 4, it can be stated that cluster 1 companies are far more standardized than cluster 3 companies. Cluster 2 companies are only a little bit less standardized than cluster 1 enterprises. This result also corresponds to the cluster characterization given before according to the result of the classical cluster analysis procedure using the factor scores.

Factor 4, personal interaction, shows especially high values within cluster 1, less in cluster 2 and hardly any value in cluster 3 companies. Therefore, personal interaction really marks global companies. This factor includes normative coordination mechanisms, but the normative point of view has often been brushed off in international marketing and management literature. Therefore, our empirical study provides new evidence that it plays a major role in a globalizing corporate world.

Hypotheses

The hypotheses presented in the theoretical part of the work were analysed on the next step. The results are presented in detail below and summarized in Table 4.27.

Hypothesis 1a could not be confirmed: there is no empirical evidence that a group of companies showing high global integration and low local adaptation exists. Only the group that is highly localized and, in parallel, also highly integrated could be proved (cf. results of the cluster analysis). This result is contradictory to considerations in the literature, where the latter group of companies (often named 'transnationals') are seen as the highest 'degree' of foreign activity and are clearly separated from the first group (see for example Bartlett, 1986; and Ghoshal and Bartlett, 1998). Probably the difficulties in defining the construct differences in theory arise from the fact that there is no difference in practice. There is just one cluster of fully globalized companies (represented by cluster 1; cf. results of the cluster analysis), another of typically multinational companies, and a cluster of beginners mainly characterized through low parameter values and only a certain degree of integration.

Cluster 1 companies, which are globally integrated and localized, form the largest group ($n = 62$) in contrast to cluster 2 ($n = 55$) and cluster 3 ($n = 13$). Therefore, hypothesis 1b, that few transnational companies exist, cannot be confirmed.

Hypothesis 2 was that a category would exist to include companies characterized by high local adaptation and decentralization. This proposition was confirmed in the results of the cluster analysis, because cluster 2 brings out exactly this factor as the most important one, determining the whole category. This confirms the theoretical considerations regarding multinational companies, that is, national adaptation/responsiveness, made by Beamish *et al.* (2000), Doz (1986), Ghoshal and Bartlett (1998), Hamel and Prahalad (1985), Martinez and Jarillo (1989) or Porter (1993) for example.

Hypothesis 3, that coordination increases during the development of a company's operations from national to global, could not be proved in the factor analysis and results of the cluster analysis. Coordination could not be identified as a single factor determining the degree of corporate globalization, but it is included in the dimension 'standardization/coordination'. This factor 'standardization/coordination' shows the highest parameter values within cluster 1, that is, the fully globalized category, and moderately high values within cluster 2, the multinational group.

The influence of the kind of industry on the LoCG was the subject matter of hypothesis 4. In this research, no influence of the industry could be detected. Both a cross tabulation of companies' own statements regarding globalization with their industry, as well as the cross tabulation of the single clusters with the cluster demographics brought the same result:[60] no significant influence could be found. As there were again some cells with counts below 5, the χ^2 test is not fully reliable for the categories 'textile industry', 'telecommunications' and 'computer and IT'. The other results are reliable. This of course challenges all measurement approaches based on the industry level (for example the approaches from Kobrin, 1991; Kim and Williamson, 1997; or Montgomery and Yip, 2000; Morrison and Roth, 1992; Makhija), because an industry's globalization level must not be valid for each company acting within that specific industry.

The companies belonging to cluster 1 use, especially, GCM programmes. This result has to be interpreted as tendentious because 40 per cent of the cells had a frequency <5 ($\chi^2 = 18.973$, $p = 0.015$), but it can nevertheless underpin the validity of the research, also because it supports the proposition made by Montgomery and Yip (2000) that a company offers GCM to global customers if it is globalized on its own (hypothesis 5). Cluster 2, the multinationals, rarely use special customer programmes. This is explicable: customer programmes need high coordination to be able to offer customers the same service wherever needed. As companies in this cluster are highly decentralized, they have no central, powerful coordination mechanisms that could manage such a programme in a consistent way. Correspondingly, multinational customers also act decentrally and do not purchase in a worldwide coordinated way, so that GCM is not an attractive instrument for customer retention. Cluster 3 does not offer special programmes at all.

Hypothesis 6 assumed that a typical order can be detected in which the value-chain activities are globalized. To test this hypothesis, the three clusters of companies found were analysed regarding differences in the globalization of their value-chain activities. Generally speaking, decisions in HRM, sales and distribution as well as logistics are made rather decentrally in cluster 1 and 2 (highly significant differences between the groups with $p = 0.000$), and centrally in cluster 3. R&D ($\chi^2 = 4.041$, $df = 2$, $p = 0.429$)[61] decisions are made centrally within all three clusters. Financial decisions are made highly centrally within cluster 3 and are significantly different from the other two groups ($\chi^2 = 27.081$, $df = 2$, $p = 0.013$).

A similar structure is visible for programme and process standardization versus adaptation. HRM ($\chi^2 = 23.421$, $df=2$, $p=0.023$) as well as sales and distribution ($\chi^2 = 40.528$, $df=2$, $p=0.001$) differ between the groups. Groups 1 and 2 balance between programme and process adaptation and standardization, and group 3 mainly standardizes. For the other areas, no differences could be found regarding the three clusters.

HRM ($\chi^2 = 34.331$, $df=2$, $p=0.011$) as well as distribution activities ($\chi^2 = 21.031$, $df=2$, $p=0.047$) are pursued highly autonomously within cluster 2 companies, and R&D is performed in a rather integrated manner within all three clusters (no significant differences between clusters could be detected; $\chi^2 = 0.559$, $df=2$, $p=0.911$). These results add to Porter's (1993) 'configuration and coordination scheme by category of activities' (presented in the theoretical part of this work on p. 22): configuration denotes activities ranging on a continuum from concentrated to dispersed. However, Porter does not state clearly which activities are performed in a concentrated manner and which are dispersed in correlation with different LoCGs. Our empirical study shows that HRM and distribution is performed in a dispersed manner within multinational companies. Marketing is, rather, performed in a more dispersed manner the higher the LoCG, whereas R&D is performed in an integrated manner within all three clusters.

These results also match partly with the theoretical considerations presented by Ohmae (1990). First, sales and distribution are performed decentrally in globalizing companies; in consequence, of course, logistics also must be performed decentrally to enable local distribution. Ohmae also stated that highly globalized companies relocated production to local markets. However, in our research, a statistically significant correlation proving this latter assumption could not be found.

Major differences could also be detected regarding the worldwide versus local use of resources. For financial resources, personnel resources and equipment, the tendency is clearly visible that cluster 3 companies use them locally, cluster 2 companies rather worldwide and cluster 1 companies mostly worldwide. These differences are all highly significant according to the results of the ANOVA: for financial resources, $\chi^2 = 82.217$, $df=2$ and $p=0.000$; for personal resources, $\chi^2 = 48.129$, $df=2$, $p=0.001$; and for equipment, $\chi^2 = 43.080$, $df=2$, $p = 0.008$.

In conclusion, hypothesis 6 could not be confirmed since no typical order of the value-chain activities could be detected. Only the R&D area seems to be not globalized at all (no differences could be detected between the three groups representing different degrees of globalization), and perhaps 'not globalizable from the companies' point of view today'. An overview of confirmed/disconfirmed hypotheses is presented in Table 4.27 based on the empirical results of our study.

Figure 4.12 summarizes the three clusters defined from the data set, including a short description of the most important cluster demographics. The factors detected by the exploratory and confirmatory factor analysis are assigned to the single clusters according to the areas on which the clusters focus most (presented *italic*). The arrows show the direction of development suggested (see also the discussion in Chapter 5, 'Limitations and future research questions').

Quantitative study: summary of results

- The level of corporate globalization can be determined by four main factors: standardization, decentralization/localization, integration,

Table 4.27　Results of the hypotheses tests

Hypothesis 1a is only partly confirmed. A group of companies having a high degree of integration and low local adaptation could not be identified. But a category that shows high global integration and localization at the same time does exist.

Hypothesis 1b is not confirmed, because more companies are assigned to the group that is globally integrated *and* localized.

Hypothesis 2 is confirmed, a group of companies is characterized by high local adaptation and decentralization.

Hypothesis 3 could not be proved. Coordination turned out not to be a single measurement dimension, but to be integrated with the standardization dimension and to have its peak in cluster 3, the international cluster.

Hypothesis 4, that the degree of corporate globalization is *not* dependent on the kind of industry the company operates in, could be confirmed.

Hypothesis 5, that companies use GCM programmes only if they are globalized, could be confirmed. Only the cluster 1 companies, that is, the fully globalized companies, indicated the use of GCM programmes.

Hypothesis 6, assuming that a typical order exists, in which the value-chain activities are globalized, could not be confirmed.

Figure 4.12 The final clusters

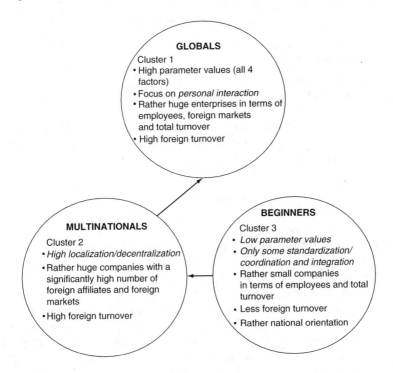

and personal interaction. These four factors consist of several items, proven to measure the LoCG:

Standardization to coordinate the enterprise units:
– Standardization of rules
– Similar knowledge application worldwide
– Established reporting processes
– Coordinated programme implementation
– Standardization of processes

Decentralization/localization:
– Local resource generation
– Profit responsibility of country managers
– Autonomous business decisions

Integration:
- International working experience
- Complementary overseas' contributions

Personal interaction:
- Worldwide vision
- Cross-functional/-national teams
- Informal people networks

- According to these factors and indicators, the data set is clustered into three groups, which represent different degrees of corporate globalization:

  Cluster 1: Globals
  Cluster 2: Multinationals
  Cluster 3: Beginners.

According to findings in the data set, globalization can be a process that companies pass through, beginning at the first stage, then becoming multinational and at last fully globalized. This process is independent from when companies start to globalize. Not every company must pass through this process; only the companies themselves will determine whether they will pass through these stages or remain in one category. There is no need or industry force – with the exception of the telecommunications industry (but here the strong globalization can be explained by the intensive merger and acquisition activities within this industry in the last few years) – to fully globalize. Therefore, the process of globalization shown is an ideal-typical way in which companies expand their foreign business. Understanding this typical development is important for:

1 companies in general to make conscious decisions about their possible development as well as about important capabilities needed to advance to the next stage; for example, to advance to become a 'global' company (where personal interaction capabilities would be of importance);
2 supplier companies using customer programmes to estimate customers' developments; that is, segmenting the customers, for deciding on GCM programme introduction, adaptation, and so on (see also the GCM literature such as Parvatiyar, 2001; Rapp,

2000; Zupancic and Senn, 2000; Wilson *et al.*, 2002; discussed in Chapter 2); and

3 customers to be able to select the right suppliers as partners that can fulfil their needs within each stage (for example, it is probably not useful for a global company to choose a national supplier to fulfil the company's worldwide product and service needs).

- The hypothesis that companies exist which are integrated and locally adapted at the same time could be proved: these companies form cluster 1. Interestingly, this cluster has the highest number of members with 62 companies. These companies are mostly huge enterprises in terms of their number of employees, number of foreign markets and total turnover. In addition, they have a high proportion of foreign turnover in relation to total turnover. The 'number-one factor' within this group of globals is 'personal interaction'.
- The use of GCM is especially recommendable for a company type belonging to cluster 1. This is so from whatever point of view – customer's or supplier's – one takes: a supplier needs a certain degree of worldwide integration to be able to satisfy customers' needs worldwide, for example, to offer the same services all over the world. Correspondingly, the customer's organizational processes and systems must support the advantages offered by GCM, otherwise the customer cannot fully benefit and will not demand GCM. A decentralized customer, for example, probably prefers nationally differentiated conditions and services, depending on the particular national environment that influences the local decisions.

Acting on the assumption that the supplier company is able to provide effective GCM, it is of major importance that it segments its customers to define to which customers to offer the GCM programme at all. Moreover, the author suggests that the company can design its GCM programme according to the characteristics of global customers, that is, cluster 1 companies. Personal interaction is the most important factor determining the fully globalized companies and should be taken into account when planning GCM for this group of customers: informal networks between employees of both sides, team-selling as a distribution instrument, and special arrangements to enhance personal contact should be included. These customers can be maintained as long-term partners if they are personally bound.

- Personal interaction is therefore one success factor for global companies, because this factor clearly distinguishes them from other companies (see also the results of our discriminant analysis). Interpreting the results of the empirical analysis, this factor 'personal interaction' enables the successful, simultaneous consolidation of local adaptation and worldwide integration and, therefore, the existence of 'transnational' companies. Therefore, companies looking for global competence should communicate a worldwide vision, deploy cross-functional and cross-national teams, and encourage informal personal networks to enhance their level of corporate globalization. As personal interaction requires experience, it seems natural that companies seeking globalization have to undergo the process described (that is, from 'beginner' to 'multinational' and then to 'global').

5
Conclusions

The central two questions of interest in this research were:

1 Which dimensions characterize companies' different levels of globalization?
2 How can these dimensions be measured in order to classify companies according to their levels of corporate globalization?

Proceeding on the definition of the construct 'global', a qualitative pre-investigation was conducted, followed by a quantitative reliability and validity examination to develop a scale measuring the level of corporate globalization. This study makes a contribution to the discussion of internationalization and globalization and its strategic implications in theory and in management practice, because it is the first attempt to specify the variables characterizing and measuring *corporate globalization* within the scope of a representative empirical study.

Theoretical implications

The discussion about globalization in the literature started years ago and many authors have tried to add to the definition of the construct 'global' as well as to the demarcation of this construct from other forms of foreign activity such as international, multinational or transnational activity. However, the diversity in theory is high, a clear demarcation does not exist and the term 'global' was rather flogged to death rather than clearly conceptualized. Therefore, the first contribution of this research lies in the proper conceptualization of the construct 'global', and the level of corporate globalization is defined as the umbrella term incorporating all different degrees of foreign activities, which are determined empirically.

The LoCG is defined by the dimensions *standardization, differentiation/localization, integration* and *personal interaction* on which companies with different LoCGs show different parameter values as shown in this empirical study. This research extends the existing measurement approaches and presents a multi-dimensional measurement approach corresponding with the complexity of the construct.

The existing measurement approaches may be adequate for a fast and simple estimation of a company's LoCG, but for a detailed segmentation approach as needed for GCM or as the basis for conscious strategic corporate planning they are inadequate. Other measurement approaches have not considered the relevant factors determining a company's LoCG in much detail, nor have they given directives for managers as how specifically to develop towards becoming a global company.

Moreover, one can clearly state that our measurement scale represents a new *customer segmentation approach* for the selection of global accounts and the differentiation of a company's customer types in general. This is based on the fact that a company's LoCG is one of the most important factors determining whether a GCM programme is needed and can be offered efficiently (cf. Millman, 1999; Montgomery and Yip, 1999; Wilson *et al.*, 2002;). In theory so far, no adequate operationalization of this segmentation approach has been presented; only the importance of this approach is stressed in the GCM literature (Millman, 1999; Montgomery and Yip, 2000; Parvatiyar and Gruen, 2001; Wilson *et al.*, 2001, 2002). The single factors and indicators determining the LoCG have been summarized in Chapter 4. The summary of the theoretical contributions of the scale already provide evidence for its practical use, which is discussed in detail below.

Managerial implications

The ability to measure a company's degree of globalization not only makes a contribution to theory, but of course also to management practice. It provides the opportunity to:

1 determine a company's strategic position, which enables in further steps the development of an adequate strategy for each stage of globalization to enhance corporate performance;[62]
2 pursue customer segmentation effectively and draw the consequences if global customer management is needed (to prevent unnecessary waste of resources); and
3 contribute to GCM programme evaluation.

The scale's practical contribution to a company's determination of its own strategic position is furthermore essential for companies to derive general strategic implications for their corporate planning and to be aware of the factors that may decide their success in their current 'cluster of action' as well as in their further and future development.

Companies belonging to cluster 1, especially, differ from the other clusters through their competence in personal interaction. These companies know how to implement cross-functional and cross-national teams as well as informal networks to manage successfully both national integration and local adaptation (normative coordination mechanisms). They communicate their global orientation in the form of a worldwide vision to both internal and external stakeholders. Especially this 'living' of a vision or orientation characterizes these companies and probably enables them to overcome organizational and structural difficulties that still bother cluster 2 and 3 companies. Communication has already been mentioned in the GCM literature as a facilitator of GCM programmes as well as of corporate globalization in general (cf. Wilson *et al.*, 2002, p. 24; and our discussion in Chapter 2). The directive for managers involved in globalizing their organizations is to ensure that personal interaction can take place. This factor can be facilitated by implementing specific informal (= personal networks) and formal (= cross-functional and -national teams as well as worldwide vision) mechanisms. The adequate functioning of these mechanisms should be examined regularly through, for example, a communication network analysis that clearly shows which employees hold key positions, perform bridging functions, and so on. On the basis of such an analysis, managers can aim at initiating contacts between the right persons to enhance the network and strengthen informal contacts.

Moreover, these cluster 1 companies have a lower level of national adaptation as well as a smaller number of foreign affiliates than cluster 2 companies. This points to the fact that cluster 1 companies have 'sacrificed' a certain degree of national differentiation and decentralization to enable the quantum of integration necessary to facilitate the implementation of personal interaction throughout the whole corporate group, and to unite the group to follow the same vision and strategic goals within all affiliates. Integration can be enhanced by ensuring that employees, especially management, have international work experience and that the overseas affiliates contribute to worldwide integrated operations.

Cluster 2 companies create their power through a distinctive concentration on differentiation/localization. These companies adapt to specific needs in each market they are working in. The high adaptation is reached by enabling local resource generation as well as autonomous business decisions, and by transferring profit responsibility to the country managers. Their degree of standardization (and therefore coordination) and integration is moderate, because each affiliate acts more or less independently from the corporate headquarters. The advantage is an absolute adaptation to local needs which can result in a competitive advantage in comparison to companies that (partly) standardize their products and neglect local demands to a certain degree. The difficulty managers face in this category is to retain an overview over the corporate group as a whole. If managers want to enhance corporate development towards cluster 1, decentralized structures within their companies have to be consolidated and knowledge about the implementation of personal interaction has to be built.

Cluster 3 companies are rather standardized, but show low parameter values in general. Standardization can be reached by standardizing rules and processes, establishing reporting processes, applying similar knowledge worldwide and coordinating programme implementation. These companies have been named 'beginners' and focus rather on the national level. This may be appropriate especially for small firms as corporate development towards higher levels of globalization absorbs a great amount of resources (financial as well as human resources and knowledge). Our empirical study has shown that only big companies (measured by the number of employees as well as annual turnover) belong to clusters 1 and 2. If cluster 3 companies are to enhance, they have to build knowledge in localization as well as integration and personal interaction to be able to reach cluster 2 or 1 levels.

Developments in the three different clusters described above are independent from the type of industry the companies operate in. Therefore, the task for managers is to focus on the company's internal situation for further development towards full globalization as well as for planning and process management on the single levels of globalization. External influences and industry pressures certainly exist and challenge a company, but cannot enhance a company's LoCG because the success factors lie *within* the company in the factors already described.

Our study has revealed the tendency that HRM, sales and distribution decisions are performed rather decentrally the higher a company's LoCG, as well as that high-LoCG companies balance between programme and process standardization and adaptation in the named areas. Therefore, companies starting to globalize should first focus on those areas.

In addition to the general strategic management issues discussed above, the measurement scale also aims at the marketing level, especially at the use of relationship management concepts. The scale enables effective customer segmentation so that an adequate GCM strategy as well as programme features can be developed for each level of corporate globalization. The objective is to ensure that the customer's organizational processes and systems support the advantages offered by GCM. The factor named by many authors as critical (Hennessey, 2001, p. 234; Wilson *et al.*, 2001), namely that the customer globally *coordinates* his purchases, could not be detected as *the* central factor because coordination was not a separate dimension but included in 'standardization'. Therefore, the focus of customer analysis should be drawn to the critical success factors detected in this research to determine which customer to serve globally. Parvatiyar and Gruen (2001) also discuss the company/supplier type as a substantial influencing factor of GCM effectiveness, but the authors could not prove the connection empirically since no operationalization of the different types was available. Our research adds to the operationalization, and in further studies the relationship to GCM effectiveness should be explored.

The results of our study clearly show that GCM is only of interest for companies belonging to the global cluster 1. This is because these companies have a number of affiliates in different markets that need to purchase, and at the same time they show the degree of integration that enables globally coordinated purchasing. Only in this constellation do the companies need a single point of contact and global service offerings, that is, the 'specialities' offered by GCM programmes. GCM programme planning and design should be adapted according to the main characterizing factor of cluster 1 companies: personal interaction. The assumption is that customers will use cross-national and -functional teams as well as informal personal networks also within the purchasing process. Therefore, the directive for global customer managers is to establish a cross-national team that reflects the customer's 'selling-team' structure as well as to enhance informal personal contacts between a company's own and the customers' employees.

A cross-national account management team can also fulfil the requirements of an integrated GCM programme design that is needed because of the global companies' (cluster 1) complexity through their claim simultaneously to integrate and adapt locally. This programme should on the one hand offer central support, and on the other hand apply to the specific needs of the affiliates. This observation corresponds with the 'fully developed GCM approach' described by Wilson, Speare and Reese (2002) that integrates all customer management activities.

Companies belonging to cluster 2 (multinationals) are not suitable for a GCM programme. The reason lies in the fact that these companies have highly decentralized and localized structures and products that make coordinated purchasing impossible. Therefore, the supplier company must not offer a GCM. The directive for managers is that *national account management* can be established with affiliates of multinational groups that operate in the supplier's markets (countries) and are profitable customers.

Cluster 3 companies (beginners) can only qualify for the supplier's national account management programme, but should be segmented regarding their profitability. A rigorous cost–benefit calculation of each customer should be the basis for any decision.

The third practical contribution of this work lies in the evaluation of GCM programmes. Here, there are different approaches to evaluate GCM programmes, and Senn's matrix of GCM (Senn and Zeier, 2002), for example, includes strategic, operational and tactical levels.

All three levels can be the object of evaluation, where the strategic level includes the measurement category 'key account selection'. Also, Wilson *etal*. (2002, pp. 180f.) state clearly that the evaluation of the global account selection process is very likely part of a performance measurement (see our discussion below on 'future research questions'). Regular evaluation of key account selection is important to perpetuate GCM effectiveness. Customers can change their organizational structures and strategies: some customers that were uninteresting in former times may have changed their classification category and can now be bound by offering them GCM.

The results of our empirical study underpin the theoretical thoughts presented in most of the GCM literature: organizational processes and systems as well as the personal factor build the basis for success (cf. model of Senn and Zeier, 2002). International work experience as well as a worldwide vision, for example, enhance a global mindset that is described as essential by Wilson, Speare and Reese (2002) for reaching corporate globalization. This is valid for both supplier and customer companies. But it is essential for suppliers offering GCM to *know* these connections, because the personal factor, for example, can be strenghtened through specific training steps and can then enable GCM effectiveness. This building process is an important stage in GCM process development, called 'developing GCM competencies' by Wilson, Speare and Reese (2002).

Our research clearly shows how, according to which factors and variables, companies can be differentiated/segmented in different degrees of corporate globalization. In addition, the variables are also success factors for companies offering GCM programmes because these enterprises should build their own competencies within these factors to adjust to their customers' levels of corporate globalization, and enable effective use and design of GCM programme features.

Limitations and future research questions

Limitations of the present research result from the following points. First, the confirmatory factor analysis results for the variables measuring the defined construct have to be interpreted with caution, since according to LISREL guidelines the sample size was fairly small. A duplicate of the empirical study using a bigger sample size would allow more conclusive results.

Second, during the empirical analysis a number of items were lost. As already mentioned in the empirical part of our work, this could be due to the fact that most literature and theory on this topic stems from American researchers and was also used as the basis of this research. The conclusion might be drawn that not all variables considered relevant for measurement in the USA are actually relevant for European companies, because American and European companies may be at different stages and showing different patterns of globalization. Therefore, a repeat study of an American-based sample might bring valuable findings. Perhaps regional differences having a strong influence on the construct might be detected, which would significantly add to theoretical knowledge.

Third, this research is a cross-sectional analysis of the sample companies' levels of corporate globalization, which implies that the construct was analysed from a static perspective. However, the results of the study seem to show that there must be a development process: if a company wants to become fully globalized, it has to pass through the stages 'beginner' and 'multinational'. This has to be, however, only a cautious statement based on the changes of the empirical values of the factors within each detected cluster of companies; it would be of major interest to measure the LoCG construct with specific consideration of the time dimension.

Future research questions lie (1) in the connection of the different degrees of corporate globalization shown in the empirical results of this work with the adequate adaptation of GCM programmes in detail, as well as (2) in the exploration of the relation of the level of corporate globalization to GCM programme performance. Regarding the first question, it would be interesting to take the cluster 1 (fully globalized) companies, as well as the cluster 2 (multinational) companies, and examine their customer management programmes. What differences or common factors might be discovered? Is there a unique practical way to design strategies according to the level of corporate globalization? A qualitative, detailed methodology could be chosen to use these empirical results and background to conceptually design different ideal-typical GCM programmes for 'globals' and 'multinationals'. These two ideal-typical programmes should offer companies basic clues and procedures as to how to use GCM for global and/or multinational customers. This could help enterprises to avoid difficulties resulting from inadequate adjustment of offered

GCM programme features to customers' and one's own levels of corporate globalization (for example, the problem of customers striving for worldwide uniform pricing agreements).

The second research area of major interest would be to explore the relation of the level of corporate globalization to the GCM programme performance. Can programme performance be enhanced by adjusting it to the different degrees of globalization? Or is GCM effective only for fully globalized companies? To be able to answer these questions, the construct 'GCM effectiveness' would first have to be defined. What constitutes effectiveness and how can it be measured? Only then could the researcher relate the customer's and the supplier's levels of corporate globalization to GCM effectiveness. Parvatiyar and Gruen (2001) tried to systematize GCM effectiveness in company and customer goals regarding financial, marketing, strategic, operational and organizational activities (see also Chapter 2 'Approaches'). However, this systematization cannot be used directly for measuring GCM effectiveness; the single dimensions at least used to explain the construct must be operationalized. Then, a causal analysis approach would probably be recommended to examine the causal connection between customer/supplier levels of corporate globalization and GCM effectiveness.

In conclusion, the research area of global customer management is an interesting field of rising importance in practice due to the increasing globalization of our world. However, it is also a still under-researched field and many questions remain to be answered. Therefore, research in this area should be encouraged to enable companies to obtain effective support in designing, implementing and further developing their GCM programmes.

Appendix 1: Questionnaire

> Project 'Levels of Corporate Globalization in Context of Global Customer Management'

Organised by Petra Kuchinka, Department of Marketing, Johannes Kepler University, Linz–July, 2002

- The following questionnaire aims to measure the level of corporate globalization according to your declarations and derive managerial implications for the development of global customer management programmes and for enhancing programme effectiveness and efficiency. If you are interested in receiving an abstract of the results, please send an email to petra.kuchinka@jku.at referring to the key word Ergebnisse (Results).
- **Please take into consideration that the questions <u>always</u> refer to the <u>international context</u> of your company.**
- To ensure practical relevance the questionnaire was developed on the basis of 13 interviews conducted with leading global customer managers of different industries.
- **Anonymity** is **guaranteed** as your answers are only analysed in an aggregated way with the answers of all other interviewees. Hence, please answer all questions as **completely** as possible.
- Please return the questionnaire by **26 July, 2002** in the enclosed return envelope. If you misplaced the envelope, please return the questionnaire to: Petra Kuchinka, Johannes Kepler University Linz, Faculty of Business, Economics and Social Science, Altenbergerstraße 69, A-4040 Linz, Austria.
- If you have any questions, please feel free to ask Petra Kuchinka, telephone +43-(0)732–2468–9407.

Many thanks for your willingness to cooperate!

1. Please mark the statement that applies best to your company (please select only one box!)

☐ Our company is *integrated* and *coordinated* worldwide in terms of decision making, programmes, implementation activities and resource application.

☐ Our company balances worldwide *integration* and *local adaptation* in terms of decision making, programmes, implementation acitivites and resource application.

☐ Our company standardizes products, procedures, processes and technology as well as business strategies across countries with very minimal adaptations, if any.

☐ Our company adapts to the national markets/countries where it is pursuing business/operating.

2. Please mark for the following statements the position on the scale that applies best to your company (international context).

2a To what extent are decisions in the following activities performed centralized (in corporate or regional headquarters) or decentralized on local country levels?

		Totally centralized			Totally decentralized		
		1	2	3	4	5	6	7
1.	Manufacturing/Production	☐	☐	☐	☐	☐	☐	☐
2.	Research and Development	☐	☐	☐	☐	☐	☐	☐
3.	Sales/Distribution	☐	☐	☐	☐	☐	☐	☐
4.	Finance/Accounting	☐	☐	☐	☐	☐	☐	☐
5.	Marketing	☐	☐	☐	☐	☐	☐	☐
6.	Human Resource Management	☐	☐	☐	☐	☐	☐	☐
7.	Logistics	☐	☐	☐	☐	☐	☐	☐

2b To what extent are programmes and processes in the following activities completely standardized across or adapted for each country?

		Completely standardized			Completely adapted		
		1	2	3	4	5	6	7
1.	Human Resource Management	☐	☐	☐	☐	☐	☐	☐
2.	Marketing	☐	☐	☐	☐	☐	☐	☐
3.	Research and Development	☐	☐	☐	☐	☐	☐	☐
4.	Finance/Accounting	☐	☐	☐	☐	☐	☐	☐
5.	Logistics	☐	☐	☐	☐	☐	☐	☐
6.	Sales/Distribution	☐	☐	☐	☐	☐	☐	☐
7.	Manufacturing/Production	☐	☐	☐	☐	☐	☐	☐

2c	To what extent the following activities are globally integrated/coordinated or conducted autonomously?						
		Totally integrated			Totally autonomous		
		1	2	3	4	5	6	7
1.	Marketing	☐	☐	☐	☐	☐	☐	☐
2.	Manufacturing/Production	☐	☐	☐	☐	☐	☐	☐
3.	Logistics	☐	☐	☐	☐	☐	☐	☐
4.	Sales/Distribution	☐	☐	☐	☐	☐	☐	☐
5.	Human Resource Management	☐	☐	☐	☐	☐	☐	☐
6.	Research and Development	☐	☐	☐	☐	☐	☐	☐
7.	Finance/Accounting	☐	☐	☐	☐	☐	☐	☐

2d To what extent your company uses the following resources cross-country to support its business (i.e. resources in one country are used for operations in another country) or local (applied to the particular country)?

		Worldwide						Local
		1	2	3	4	5	6	7
1.	Financial Resources	☐	☐	☐	☐	☐	☐	☐
2.	Human Resources	☐	☐	☐	☐	☐	☐	☐
3.	Equipments	☐	☐	☐	☐	☐	☐	☐

3. Please mark for the following statements the position on the scale from "Totally disagree" to "Totally agree" that applies best to your company (international context).

	Totally disagree					Totally agree	
In my company competitive strategies in one country are significantly affected by our competitive strategies in another country.	☐ 1	☐ 2	☐ 3	☐ 4	☐ 5	☐ 6	☐ 7
Our company has a significant number of brands that have similar images across countries.	☐ 1	☐ 2	☐ 3	☐ 4	☐ 5	☐ 6	☐ 7
In our company assets and resources are dispersed and interdependent among international organizational units.	☐ 1	☐ 2	☐ 3	☐ 4	☐ 5	☐ 6	☐ 7
Intangible assets are widely shared across countries.	☐ 1	☐ 2	☐ 3	☐ 4	☐ 5	☐ 6	☐ 7
Joint knowledge development projects are undertaken within our company involving cross-country resources.	☐ 1	☐ 2	☐ 3	☐ 4	☐ 5	☐ 6	☐ 7
Our senior management has a world view of our business operations and opportunities.	☐ 1	☐ 2	☐ 3	☐ 4	☐ 5	☐ 6	☐ 7

	Totally disagree					Totally agree	
Products are standardized wherever possible and localized wherever needed.	☐ 1	☐ 2	☐ 3	☐ 4	☐ 5	☐ 6	☐ 7
At various levels of our company, managers have international work experience.	☐ 1	☐ 2	☐ 3	☐ 4	☐ 5	☐ 6	☐ 7
Overseas operations provide complementary contributions by national units to integrated worldwide operations.	☐ 1	☐ 2	☐ 3	☐ 4	☐ 5	☐ 6	☐ 7
Knowledge developed in one country is widely shared across countries within our company.	☐ 1	☐ 2	☐ 3	☐ 4	☐ 5	☐ 6	☐ 7
The company communicates a worldwide vision to both internal and external stakeholders.	☐ 1	☐ 2	☐ 3	☐ 4	☐ 5	☐ 6	☐ 7
Our company adopts technology platform standards worldwide.	☐ 1	☐ 2	☐ 3	☐ 4	☐ 5	☐ 6	☐ 7
Our employees have access to required specific and general company information on a worldwide basis.	☐ 1	☐ 2	☐ 3	☐ 4	☐ 5	☐ 6	☐ 7
Business strategies and programmes are uniquely developed for each country by our company.	☐ 1	☐ 2	☐ 3	☐ 4	☐ 5	☐ 6	☐ 7
Country managers often seek to adopt and leverage parent company resources and strategies.	☐ 1	☐ 2	☐ 3	☐ 4	☐ 5	☐ 6	☐ 7
Global strategies are based on local inputs.	☐ 1	☐ 2	☐ 3	☐ 4	☐ 5	☐ 6	☐ 7
Marketing and sales function are highly decentralized at the country management level.	☐ 1	☐ 2	☐ 3	☐ 4	☐ 5	☐ 6	☐ 7
There is frequent communication among national units to align each others' activities.	☐ 1	☐ 2	☐ 3	☐ 4	☐ 5	☐ 6	☐ 7
Individual country assets and resources are managed on a centralized basis within our company.	☐ 1	☐ 2	☐ 3	☐ 4	☐ 5	☐ 6	☐ 7
Local country units actively participate in the overall strategic planning and budgeting process of our company.	☐ 1	☐ 2	☐ 3	☐ 4	☐ 5	☐ 6	☐ 7
The local governance of country subsidiaries is autonomous and HQ has limited influence on it, if any.	☐ 1	☐ 2	☐ 3	☐ 4	☐ 5	☐ 6	☐ 7

	Totally disagree						Totally agree
Procurement function within our company is centralized.	☐ 1	☐ 2	☐ 3	☐ 4	☐ 5	☐ 6	☐ 7
Cross-functional and cross-national teams (both real and virtual) for specific projects exist in our company.	☐ 1	☐ 2	☐ 3	☐ 4	☐ 5	☐ 6	☐ 7
Country managers are required to generate their own resources for ongoing business operations within their country.	☐ 1	☐ 2	☐ 3	☐ 4	☐ 5	☐ 6	☐ 7
Our company employees have shared values and common culture around the world.	☐ 1	☐ 2	☐ 3	☐ 4	☐ 5	☐ 6	☐ 7
Minimal interference is exerted from headquarters for managing individual country operations.	☐ 1	☐ 2	☐ 3	☐ 4	☐ 5	☐ 6	☐ 7
Our company actively pursues any unique local country opportunities.	☐ 1	☐ 2	☐ 3	☐ 4	☐ 5	☐ 6	☐ 7
National/regional/global goals within our company are clearly stated and aligned with each other.	☐ 1	☐ 2	☐ 3	☐ 4	☐ 5	☐ 6	☐ 7
Our company's organizational structure in one country is a mirror image of the structure in another country.	☐ 1	☐ 2	☐ 3	☐ 4	☐ 5	☐ 6	☐ 7
Our company's products/services are fully adapted for each market.	☐ 1	☐ 2	☐ 3	☐ 4	☐ 5	☐ 6	☐ 7
Our company's view about customer needs, wants and behaviour across countries is same.	☐ 1	☐ 2	☐ 3	☐ 4	☐ 5	☐ 6	☐ 7
Assets/capabilities in each national market are considered unique to that country and rarely utilized for other country operations.	☐ 1	☐ 2	☐ 3	☐ 4	☐ 5	☐ 6	☐ 7
Our company affiliates in individual countries rarely share the knowledge developed by them with other company affiliates.	☐ 1	☐ 2	☐ 3	☐ 4	☐ 5	☐ 6	☐ 7
Our company's products are highly standardized across countries with very minimal adaptations, if any.	☐ 1	☐ 2	☐ 3	☐ 4	☐ 5	☐ 6	☐ 7
Country managers in our company have full profit and loss responsibilities related to all functions of the business.	☐ 1	☐ 2	☐ 3	☐ 4	☐ 5	☐ 6	☐ 7
Our business strategies across countries are very similar to each other.	☐ 1	☐ 2	☐ 3	☐ 4	☐ 5	☐ 6	☐ 7

	Totally disagree					Totally agree	
Rules and procedures in our company are standardized wherever possible, and localized wherever needed.	☐ 1	☐ 2	☐ 3	☐ 4	☐ 5	☐ 6	☐ 7
Application of knowledge in all countries within our company is undertaken in a highly similar manner.	☐ 1	☐ 2	☐ 3	☐ 4	☐ 5	☐ 6	☐ 7
Country managers make autonomous business decisions relative to their individual operations.	☐ 1	☐ 2	☐ 3	☐ 4	☐ 5	☐ 6	☐ 7
Significant decisions for regional and national operations are centralized within our company.	☐ 1	☐ 2	☐ 3	☐ 4	☐ 5	☐ 6	☐ 7
Performance measurement metrics are similar across various national units in our company.	☐ 1	☐ 2	☐ 3	☐ 4	☐ 5	☐ 6	☐ 7
Informal networks among people across countries within our company exist to support programme implementation.	☐ 1	☐ 2	☐ 3	☐ 4	☐ 5	☐ 6	☐ 7
Country managers have full authority in making procurement decisions for their entities.	☐ 1	☐ 2	☐ 3	☐ 4	☐ 5	☐ 6	☐ 7
There are established processes for reporting programme progress and feedback from various national units.	☐ 1	☐ 2	☐ 3	☐ 4	☐ 5	☐ 6	☐ 7
Our company has well-defined roles for individuals involved in national/ international operations.	☐ 1	☐ 2	☐ 3	☐ 4	☐ 5	☐ 6	☐ 7
Country managers are free to cooperate or collaborate among themselves without seeking HQ approval.	☐ 1	☐ 2	☐ 3	☐ 4	☐ 5	☐ 6	☐ 7
Programme implementation and the related decisions are coordinated across countries.	☐ 1	☐ 2	☐ 3	☐ 4	☐ 5	☐ 6	☐ 7
Procedures, processes and technology applied across country locations within our company are highly standardized and minimal adaptations are permitted.	☐ 1	☐ 2	☐ 3	☐ 4	☐ 5	☐ 6	☐ 7

4. To what extent is your company global according to your opinion? (Please select only one box!)

Global Aspirant					Fully Globalized	
☐ 1	☐ 2	☐ 3	☐ 4	☐ 5	☐ 6	☐ 7

5.	Please make general specifications for company classification.
5a	Your position within the company is... (multiple nominations possible) ☐ CEO ☐ International Key Account Manager ☐ Head of Sales ☐ Global Key Account Manager ☐ Marketing Executive ☐ Other, please specify: .... ☐ National Key Account .... Manager
5b	In which industry does your company operate (multiple nominations possible)? ☐ Automobile Industry ☐ Computer ☐ Textile Industry ☐ Chemical Industry Industry and IT ☐ Telecommunications ☐ Foods and Beverages ☐ Engineering ☐ Other, please specify: Industry ....
5c	On how many foreign markets (on country-basis) does your company pursue business/operate? .... (number of) countries
5d	When did your company start to operate on foreign markets? ....
5e	Do you pursue any special programme for customers? (If no, please go to question 5 g) ☐ Yes ☐ No
5f	If 'yes', which programme? ☐ National account management ☐ Global account management ☐ International account ☐ Other: .... management
5g	What percentage of the sales volume 2001 is generated through international activities? .... € millions
5h	The worldwide sales volume 2001 is... .... € millions
5i	Please indicate the number of employees engaged worldwide: ....
5k	How many nationalities are represented within your company? ....
5l	Please indicate your number of foreign affiliates:	5m Please indicate the number of total affiliates: ....

Appendix 2: NVivo Chart

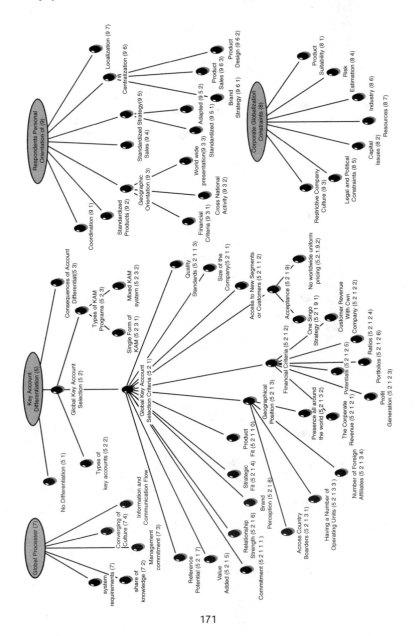

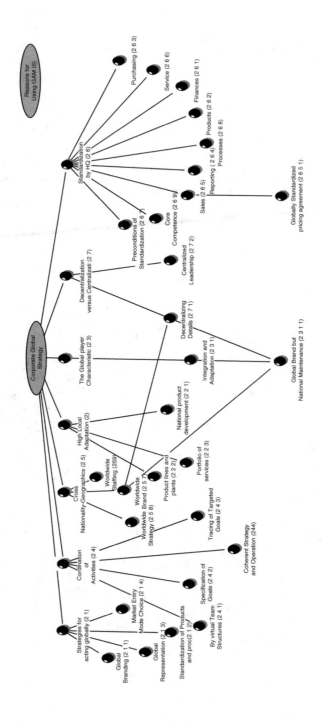

173

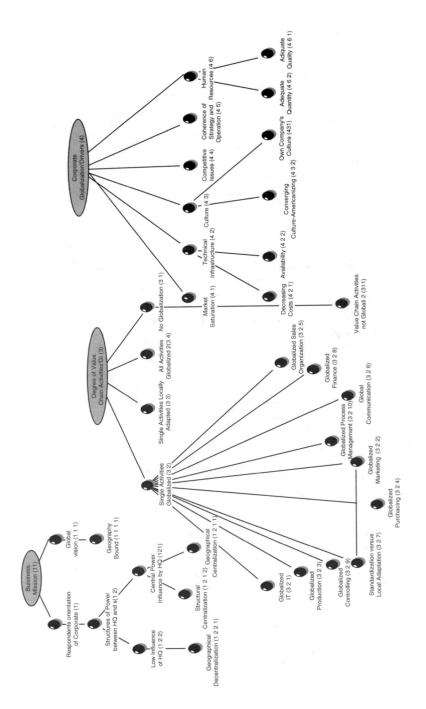

Notes

1   From this point of view, the aim of this research is to measure a customer's *'degree of internal coordination of purchasing'*. However, as it is not empirically proven that this dimension is the main characteristic that differentiates global customers from others, the measurement scale should be constructed on the basis of dimensions that are generally assumed to define global companies in the literature. Therefore, the scale is named 'levels of corporate globalization'.

2   Cf. the definition of Bruhn (2001, p. 9): 'Relationship marketing includes all analysis, planning, implementation and controlling methods, which serve the initiation, stabilization, intensification and recovery of business relationships with ... the company's customers with the aim of *mutual value'*.

3   Customer retention contributes to distribution assurance, implicates increased purchasing frequency and cross-selling potential as well as an increased willingness to pay because of risk reduction (cf. Bruhn, 2001, p. 3).

4   Transnational corporations.

5   Cf. Dunning (1977); Dunning and Pearce (1981).

6   Non-equity forms of international cooperation (NEC) are defined as 'inter-corporate, international business operations that lie in a grey area between arms-length trade and traditional FDI' (Oman, 1989, p. 9, cited in Nunnenkamp *et al.*, 1994, p. 27) This definition particularly means licensing agreements, production-sharing arrangements, international subcontracting or franchising contracts and turnkey projects as well as – broadly defined – joint ventures with minor foreign equity stakes (Contractor and Lorange, 1988, pp. 5ff.). Often tangible or intangible assets are delivered by a foreign enterprise to a local one, while full or majority ownership is local.

7   The terms global account management and global customer management are used interchangeably to designate the same concept.

8   Cross-subsidization is defined as the use of financial resources that are gained in one part of the world for fighting competition in another part. (Hamel and Prahalad, 1993, pp. 130f.).

9   Scope economies can emerge because the cost of joint production of two or more products can be less than the cost of producing them separately. This can occur, for example, through shared physical assets, shared external relations or shared learning (Ghoshal, 1993, p. 184).

10 This is the reason why the terms internationalization and globalization are demarcated and not used synonymously.

11 Criticized by Ramaswamy, Kroeck and Penforth (1996).

12 The terms internationalization and globalization are used synonymously here accordingly to literature interpretations.

13 Mergers and acquisitions are also of importance for all other variables that can be measured in this connection, but are named here only for reasons of completeness and are not considered further in this study.

14 The terms CRM and relationship marketing should be defined. According to the author, both approaches follow the same strategic objectives and strategies, and therefore one could equate strategic relationship marketing with strategic CRM. However, speaking generally of CRM, it always includes a strong technical component, i.e. computer- supported processing of customer data, which acts as a complement to the strategic viewpoint.

15 Often synonymously named global account management (GAM).

16 Interested readers can look at further reading: Kulessa, Frank and Stangl (1999); Millman (1999); Montgomery and Yip (2000); Wilson *et al.* (2001); and others.

17 Cf. general literature on relationship marketing: Cram (1994); Christopher *et al.* (1991); Henning-Thurau and Hansen (2000); Payne (1995); Sheth and Parvsyiyar (2000).

18 The terms global account management and global customer management are used interchangeably.

19 This simple one-dimensional case has also been used in the example presented in Figure 3.1 describing the level of corporate globalization and company site.

20 As constructs can therefore consist of a number of sub-constructs, namely dimensions, these sub-constructs are subsumed in this work in the term 'construct'. This practice was already pursued, for example, by Werani (1998, pp. 81f.).

21 Not completely without any errors.

22 The example used is based on the form of reflective indicators.

23 Detailed descriptions of random and systematic errors are given by Carmines and Zeller (1979), for example.

24 For formal presentation of this equation see for example Churchill (1979), p. 65.

25 Cf. for example Backhaus *et al.* (1994); Homburg (1995); Werani (1998).

26 According to a suggestion from Churchill (1979, p. 68), which was for example already tested in Werani (1998), the item-to-total correlations are used in a *relative* and not an absolute sense.

27 This approach is based on a linear structural equations model (cf. Backhaus *et al.*, 1994, pp. 324, 327).

28 Detailed information is not given in this work since recently very much has been written about the LISREL approach and the aim is only to use this methodological approach, not to contribute to any further explanations or theoretical descriptions. The reader is therefore referred to, for example, Diamantopoulos (1994, pp. 225ff.); Bagozzi and Fornell (1982); Jöreskog and Sörbom (1996); Werani (1998, pp. 96ff.); for methodological explanations.

29 This focus implies the use of the two-step modelling approach suggested by Anderson and Gerbing (1982, p. 453) because this approach states

that the correct specification of the measurement model is the basis for the following analysis of the causal relations between the latent variables. If the measurement model shows a poor fit, it could be compensated for by the structural model and show an adequate fit at the end.

As the aim is to gain information about the reliability and validity of the measurement scale, the aspect of scale testing is as important as the analysis of causal relations between the latent variables. This justifies the choice of the two-step approach also *vis-à-vis* critics favouring a one-step modelling approach (i.e. to integrate the measurement and structural model and evaluate both simultaneously) to utilize the strength of LISREL, namely the connection of theory and data (see Hulland, Chow and Lam, 1996, p. 185).

30 The multifactor solution was soon used after the original unifactor analysis development.

31 r is a positive constant. If $r = 1$, one speaks of the L_1-norm (City block); if $r = 2$, it is the L_2-norm (Euclidean distance).

32 For detailed description of the single methods, the reader is referred to pertinent literature, for example Backhaus *et al.* (2000, pp. 355ff.).

33 Accurately, these independent variables should be called quasi-metric, because in fact they have an ordinal measurement level represented through the seven-point Likert scale. However, as the distances between the single scale grades are configured identically (graphical presentation in the questionnaire), it is legitimate to use them as interval-scaled variables. This approach is regularly used in empirical work and can be found, for example, in the work of Jensen (2001, p. 98).

34 For detailed information on other possible criteria, the interested reader is referred to pertinent literature, as for example Backhaus *et al.* (2000).

35 Many authors writing on qualitative research, for example Miles and Huberman (1994, p. 41), endorse the supposition that qualitative data helps designing a quantitative study by aiding with conceptual development and instrumentation.

36 Different industries were chosen to get a broad perspective on the construct 'global' in order to develop standard indicators relevant for the measurement of the LoCG in different industries. Of course, these indicators can vary in intensity or degree according to different industries or companies.

37 SAMA (Strategic Account Management Association) Best Practice Forum in Zürich, 5 February 2002.

38 As far as one can speak of 'validity' when talking about qualitative research.

39 Austrian companies were overrepresented in this study for cost-efficiency reasons (their easy accessibility).

40 A number that was not surprising since a major part of the investigation took place in summer time and the general response rate has already been low for years. The questionnaires were filled out sufficiently and the return is high enough to be able to analyse the data, as planned, with exploratory and confirmatory factor analysis.

41 Other criteria such as turnover, for example, could not be added for the representativity test as the according data could not be assigned to the companies chosen.

42 Which could be expected due to the Hoppenstedt® data material.

43 The reason why these percentages add up to more than 100 per cent lies in the fact that some contact persons are assigned to several functional positions. This was especially the case in small companies, where people fulfil multiple tasks and positions at once.

44 Foreign activities are defined as the sum of exports and foreign production minus reimports (cf. Stopford *et al.*, 1992).

45 Supposing that the questions probably did not fit these companies: those companies eliminated were very small companies in terms of turnover and number of employees, had no foreign affiliates and worked on very few – if any – foreign markets. They only mentioned exporting goods. Therefore, these companies did not fulfil the selection criteria, i.e. at least one foreign affiliate, and were included by mistake.

46 The single linkage cluster approach is especially adequate to identify outliers (Backhaus *et al.*, 2000, pp. 359, 367).

47 LISREL is based on the assumption of dependencies and causalities which is the same principle used within the principal-axis method. The aim of the principal-axis method is to explain the variables' variances through hypothetical factors which implicates a differentiation between communalities and single residual variance, i.e. correlations are interpreted causally and the starting values of the communalities are always <1. On the other hand, the principal-component method does not differentiate or interpret causally and starts analysis with a given eigenvalue of 1 (Backhaus *et al.*, 2000, p. 285).

48 The guideline was also set by Field (2000, p. 437).

49 According to Backhaus *et al.* (2000, p. 266), although some authors for example set $R > 0.8$ as the borderline for high correlation (cf. Field, 2000, p. 445).

50 Used to test the hypothesis of whether the sample is descended from a population with uncorrelated variables (Backhaus *et al.*, 2000, p. 267).

51 The maximum value in this data set is 1.37 for the skewness and 1.27 for the kurtosis.

52 The limit was set before with $\alpha \geq 0.70$.

53 As the calculation formulas of all missing measures are based on the degrees of freedom.

54 As is known, the level of this coefficient is also positively dependent on the number of indicators (cf. Carmines and Zeller, 1979, p. 45f). One could therefore expect a rather low value.

55 For detailed descriptions of the measures' functionality, see for example Homburg (1995); Homburg and Giering (1996); or Anderson and Gerbing (1982).

56 See also the discussion in Chapter 2, 'Measurement Dimensions of Globalization'.

57 The reasoning behind this measure was discussed in Chapter 3.

58   The resources do not necessarily include R&D, which is often still managed by the headquarters.
59   SME = small and medium-sized enterprises
60   For the automobile industry, the homogeneity chi-squared test of the cross-tabulation was $\chi^2 = 0.193$, $df = 2$, $p = 0.908$; for chemicals, $\chi^2 = 0.276$, $df = 2$, $p = 0.871$; for beverages and food, $\chi^2 = 2.354$, $df = 2$, $p = 0.308$; for computers, $\chi^2 = 1.899$, $df = 2$, $p = 0.387$; for engineering, $\chi^2 = 2.304$, $df = 2$, $p = 0.316$; for textiles, $\chi^2 = 4.263$, $df = 2$, $p = 0.119$; for telecommunications, $\chi^2 = 0.244$, $df = 2$, $p = 0.885$, and for the miscellaneous category, $\chi^2 = 1.704$, $df = 2$ and $p = 0.427$.
61   Method used: multiple t-value comparison with ANOVA.
62   The development of adequate strategies is seen as an important next step, but was not considered as the aim of this work and is therefore not discussed further.

Bibliography

Adler, N. and Bartholomew, S. (1992) 'Managing Globally Competent People', *Academy of Management Executive*, vol. 6 (3), 52–65.

Allen, T.J. (1984) *Managing the Flow of Technology: Technology Transfer and the Dissemination of Technological Information within the R&D Organization*, 1st paperback printing (Cambridge, Mass. and London: MIT Press).

Andersen, O. (1993) 'On the Internationalization Process of Firms: A Critical Analysis', *Journal of International Business Studies*, vol. 24 (2), 209–31.

Anderson, J.C. and Gerbing, D.W. (1982) 'Some Methods for Respecifying Measurement Modes to Obtain Unidimensional Construct Measurement', *Journal of Marketing Research*, vol. 19 (November), 453–60.

Arnold, D., Birkinshaw, J. and Toulan, O. (1999) 'Implementing Global Account Management in Multinational Corporations', *Thexis*, 4/1999, St Gallen, 14–17.

Ashkenas, R., Ulrich, D., Jick, T. and Kerr, S. (1995) *The Boundaryless Organization* (San Francisco, Cal.: Jossey-Bass).

Atac, O.A. (1986) 'International Experience Theory and Global Strategy', *International Marketing Review*, vol. 3 (4), 52–61.

Backhaus, K., Erichson, B., Plinke, W. and Weiber, R. (1994) *Multivariate Analysemethoden: Eine anwendungsorientierte Einführung*, 7th edn (Berlin: Springer).

Backhaus, K., Erichson, B., Plinke, W. and Weiber, R. (2000) *Multivariate Analysemethoden: Eine anwendungsorientierte Einführung*, 9th edn (Berlin: Springer).

Bagozzi, R.P. (1994) *Principles of Marketing Research* (Cambridge/Oxford: Blackwell).

Bagozzi, R. and Fornell, C. (1982) 'Theoretical Concepts, Measurement and Meaning', in C. Fornell (ed.), *A Second Generation of Multivariate Analysis*, (New York: Prager Publishers), 24–38.

Bartlett, C.A. (1986) 'Building and Managing the Transnational: The New Organizational Challenge', in M.E. Porter (ed.), *Competition in Global Industries* (Boston, Mass.: Harvard Business School Press).

Bartlett, C.A., Doz, Y. and Hedlund, G. (1990) *Managing the Global Firm* (New York: Routledge).

Bartlett, C.A. and Ghoshal, S. (1987) 'Managing Across Borders: New Organizational Responses', *Sloan Management Review*, vol. 29 (1), 43–53.

Bartlett, C.A. and Ghoshal, S. (1988) 'Organizing for Worldwide Effectiveness: The Transnational Solution', *California Management Review*, vol. 31 (1), 54–74.

Bartlett, C.A. and Ghoshal, S. (1989) *Managing Across Borders: The Transnational Solution* (Boston, Mass.: Harvard Business School Press).

Bartlett, C.A. and Ghoshal, S. (1990) 'The Multinational Corporation as an Inter-organization Network', *Academy of Management Review*, vol. 15 (4), 603–25.

Bartlett, C.A. and Ghoshal, S. (1995) 'Changing the Role of Top Management: Beyond Systems to People', *Harvard Business Review*, May/June, 132–42.

Bazeley, P. (1999) 'The Bricoleur With a Computer: Piecing Together Qualitative and Quantitative Data', *Qualitative Health Research*, vol. 9 (2) (London: Sage), 279–87.

Bazeley, P. and Richards, L. (2000) *The NVivo Qualitative Project Book* (London: Sage).

Beamish, P.W., Morrison, A.J., Rosenzweig, P.M. and Inkpen, A.C. (2000) *International Management: Text and Cases*, 4th edn (Boston, Mass.: Irwin McGraw-Hill).

Beck, U. (1997) *Was ist Globalisierung?* 3rd edn (Frankfurt am Main: Suhrkamp).

Bellak, C., Fischer, O., Podesser, P., Rieger, B. and Schönhofer, P. (1989a) *Internationalisierung*, vol. I, 'Die Internationalisierung der österreichischen Industrie: Eine erste Standortbestimmung' (Wien: Industriewissenschaftliches Institut).

Bellak, C., Fischer, O., Podesser, P., Rieger, B. and Schönhofer, P. (1989b) *Internationalisierung*, vol. II, '17 aus 338 – Internationalisierungsstrategien österreichischer Unternehmen' (Wien: Industriewissenschaftliches Institut).

Belz, Ch., Müllner, M. and Zupancic, D. (2001) *Performances and Organizational Structures in International Industrial Key Account Management* (St Gallen: University, Institute of Marketing and Retailing).

Bennett, J.W. and Dahlberg, K.A. (1993) *Institutions, Social Organizations, and Cultural Values; The Earth as Transformed by Human Action* (New York: Cambridge University Press), 69–85.

Birkinshaw, J., Toulan, O. and Arnold, D. (2001) 'Global Account Management in Multinational Corporations: Theory and Evidence', *Journal of International Business Studies*, vol. 32 (2), 231–248.

Bollen, K.A. (1989) *Structural Equations with Latent Variables*, Wiley series in probability and mathematical statistics (New york: John Wiley & Sons).

Bowonder, B., Yadav S. and Sunil B. (2000) *R&D Spending Patterns of Global Firms*, Research Technology Management, vol. 43 (5) 40–56.

Brewster, C. and Harris, H. (1999) *International HRM* (London: Routledge).

Bruhn, M. (2001) *Relationship Marketing: Das Management von Kundenbeziehungen* (München: Vahlen).

Bühl, A. and Zöfel, P. (2000) SPSS Version 10: Einfuhring in die moderne Datananalyse unter Windows (7th edn), Aujlage (Reading, Mass.: Addison-Wesley).

Cantwell, J. (1989) 'The Globalization of Technology: What Remains of the Product-Cycle Model', in A. Chandler, P. Hagstrom, O. Solvell and O. Oxford (eds), *The Dynamic Firm* (Oxford: Oxford University Press), 263–88.

Carmines, E.G. and Zeller, R.A. (1979) *Reliability and Validity Assessment* (London: Sage).

Carnap, R. (1953) 'Testability and Meaning', in H. Feigel and M. Brodbeck (eds), *Readings in the Philosophy of Science* (New York: Appleton-Century-Crofts), 47–92.

Carpenter, M.A. Fredrickson, J.W. (2001) 'Top Management Teams, Global Strategic Posture and the Moderating Role of Uncertainty', *Academy of Management Journal*, vol. 44 (3), 533–45.

Cavusgil, S.T. (1982) 'Some Observations on the Relevance of Critical Variables for Internationalization Stages', in M.R. Czinkota and G. Tesar (eds), *Export Management – An International Context* (New York: Praeger Publishers), 276–86.

Cavusgil, S.T. (1992) *International Marketing: An Annotated Bibliography* (Chicago, Ill.: American Marketing Association).

Christopher, M., Payne, A. and Ballantyne, D. (1991) *Relationship Marketing: Bringing Quality, Customer Service and Marketing together* (Oxford: Butterworth-Heinemann).

Churchill, G. (1979) 'A Paradigm for Developing Better Measures of Marketing Constructs', *Journal of Marketing Research*, vol. 16, 64–73.

Collis, D.J. (1991) 'A Resource-based Analysis of Global Competition: The Case of the Bearings Industry', *Strategic Management Journal*, vol. 12 (special issue), 49–68.

Contractor, F.J. and Lorange, P. (1988) 'Why Should, Firms Cooperate? The Strategy and Economic Basis for Cooperative Ventures', F.J. Contractor and P. Lorange (eds), *Cooperative Strategies in International Business* (Lexington, Mass.: Lexington Books), 3–30.

Cram, T. (1994) *The Power of Relationship Marketing: Keeping Customers for Life* (London: Pitman).

Daniels, J.D. and Bracker, J. (1989) 'Profit Performance: Do Foreign Operations Make a Difference?' *Management International Review*, vol. 29, 46–56.

Daniels, J.D. and Radebaugh, L.H. (1992) *International Business*; 6th edn (Reading, Mass.: Addison-Wesley).

Daroczi, Z. (2000) 'Review: Aulakh P.S. and M.G. Schechter (eds): *Rethinking Globalization(s): From Corporate Transnationalism to Local Interventions, Journal of International Marketing*, 8(4).

Davidow, W. and Malone, M. (1992) *The Virtual Corporation* (New York: Harper & Row).

Day, E., Fox, R. and Huszagh, S.M. (1988) 'Segmenting the Global Market for Industrial Goods: Issues and Implications', *International Marketing Review*, vol. 5 (3), 14–27.

Diamantopoulos, A. (1994) 'Modelling with LISREL: A Guide for the Uninitiated', G.J. Hooley and M.K. Hussey (eds), *Quantitative Methods in Marketing* (London: The Dryden Press).

Doney, P.M. and Cannon, J.P. (1997) 'An Examination of the Nature of Trust in Buyer–Seller Relationships', *Journal of Marketing*, vol. 61 (2) (April 1997), 35–51.

Doz, Y.L. (1986) *Strategic Management in Multinational Corporations* (Oxford: Pergamon).

Drucker, P. (1989) *The New Realities* (New York: Harper & Row).

Dunning, J.H. (1973) 'The Determinants of International Production', *Oxford Economic Press*, no. 25, 289–336.

Dunning, J.H. (1977) 'Trade, Location of Economic Activity and the MNE: A Search for an Eclectic Approach', in B. Ohlin, P.O. Hessel-Born and P.M. Wijkman (eds), *The International Allocation of Economic Activity* (London: Macmillan), 395–418.

Dunning, J.H. (1988) *Explaining International Production* (London: Unwin Hyman).

Dunning, J.H. (1993) *Multinational Enterprises and the Global Economy* (Wokingham: Addison-Wesley).

Dunning, J.H. (1995) 'Reappraising the Eclectic Paradigm in an Age of Alliance Capitalism', *Journal of International Business Studies*, vol. (3), 461–91.

Dunning, J.H. and Pearce, R. (1981) *The World's Largest Industrial Enterprises* (London: Gower).

Dymsza, W.A. (1984) 'Global Strategic Planning: A Model and Recent Developments', *Journal of International Business Studies*, Fall, 169–83.

Evans, P., Doz, Y. and Laurent, Y.A. (1989) *Human Resource Management in International Firms* (Basingstoke: Macmillan – Palgrave).

Field, A. (2000) *Discovering Statistics: Using SPSS for Windows* (London: Sage).

Fisher, R.A. (1936) 'The use of multiple measurements in taxonomic problems', *Annets of Eupenics*, 7, 179–88, Cambridge: Cambridge University Press.

Fraedrich, J., Herndon, N.C. and Ferrell, O.C. (1995) 'A Values Comparison of Future Managers from West Germany and the United States', in Salah S. Hassan and Erdener Kayak (eds), *Globalization of Consumer Markets* (New York: International Business Press), 303–25.

Fritz, W. (1995) *Unternehmenserfolg: Grund bogen einer Empirischen Untersuchung* (2nd edn) (Stuttgart: Schäffer-Poeschel).

Gerbing, D. and Anderson, J. (1988) 'An Updated Paradigm for Scale Development Incorporating Unidimensionality and its Assessment', *Journal of Marketing Research*, vol. 25, 186–92.

Gestrin, M., Knight, R.F. and Rugman, A.M. (1999a) *The Templeton Global Performance Index* (Oxford: Templeton College Oxford), 36.

Gestrin, M., Knight, R.F. and Rugman, A.M. (1999b) *Templeton Global Performance index* (Oxford: Templeton College Oxford), 31.

Giddens, A. (1990) *The Consequences of Modernity* (Cambridge: Polity Press).

Giddens, A. (1995) *Konsequenzen der Moderne* (Frankfurt am Main: Suhrkamp).

Giddens, A. (1999) *Runaway World: How Globalization is Reshaping our Lives* (London: Profile Books).

Ghoshal, S. (1987) 'Global Strategy: An Organizing Framework', *Strategic Management Journal*, vol. 8 (5), 425–40.

Ghoshal, S. (1993) 'Global strategy: an organizing framework', in D.J. Lecraw, A.J. Morrison and J.H. Dunning (eds), *Transnational Corporations and Business Strategy*, vol. 4 (London and New York: Routledge).

Ghoshal, S. and Bartlett, C.A. (1998) *Managing Across Borders: The Transnational Solution* (London: Random House Business Books).

Hakansson, H. (1982) *International Marketing and Purchasing of Goods: An Interaction Approach* (New York: John Wiley & Sons).

Hamel, G. and Prahalad, C.K. (1985) 'Do You Really Have a Global Strategy?', *Harvard Business Review*, July/August, 139–48.

Hamel, G. and Prahalad, C.K. (1993) 'Do you Really Have a Global Strategy?', in D.J. Lecraw, A.J. Morrison and J.H. Dunning (eds), *Transnational Corporations: and Business Strategy*, 123–37.

Hassel, A., Hoepner, M., Kurdelbusch, A., Rehder, B. and Zugehoer, R. (2000) *Two Dimensions of the Internationalization of Firms* (Cologne: Max Planck Institute for the Study of Societies).

Hedlund, G. (1986) 'The Hypermodern MNC – A Heterarchy?', *Human Resource Management*, Spring, vol. 25 (1), 9–27.

Heenan, D.A. and Perlmutter, H.V. (1979) *Multinational Organization Development – A Social Architectural Perspective* (Reading, Mass.: Addison-Wesley).

Heidelberger Club für Wirtschaft und Kultur e.V. (eds), (1997) *Globalisierung: Der Schritt in ein neues Zeitalter* (Berlin.: Springer).

Hennessey, H.D. (2001) 'Managing Global Customers', in P. Kirkbride (eds), *Globalization: The External Pressures* (Chichester: John Wiley & Sons).

Hennig-Thurau, Th. and Hansen, U. (2000) *Relationship Marketing: Gaining Competitive Advantage Through Customer Satisfaction and Customer Retention* (Berlin: Springer).

Hildebrandt, L. (1984) 'Kausalanalyztische Validierung in der Marketing forschung', *Marketing-Zeitschrift fur Forschung und Praxis*, vol. 6 (1), 41–51.

Hildebrandt, L. and Homburg, Ch. (1998) *Die Kausalanalyse: ein Instrument der empirischen betriebswirtschaftlichen Forschung* (Stuttgart: Schäffer-Poeschel).

Hilti Group (2002) *Corporate Case Study*, SAMA Best Practice Forum 2002, Zurich, 5 February 2002.

Homburg, Ch. (1995) *Kundennähe von Industriegüterunternehmen: Konzeption – Erfolgsauswirkungen – Determinanten* (Wiesbaden: Gabler).

Holland, J., Chow, Y. and Lam, S. (1996) 'Use of Causal Models in Marketing Research: A Review', *International Journal of Research in Marketing*, vol. 13 (2), 181–97.

Homburg, Ch. and Giering, A. (1996) 'Konzeptualisierung und Operationalisierung komplexer Konstrukte: Ein Leitfaden für die Marktingforschung', *Marketing Zeitschrift Fur Forschung und Praxis*, vol. 1 (1), 5–24.

Homburg, C. and Baumgartner, H. (1995) 'Beurkilung Von Kauselmodellen: Bestands-aufnahne und Ansenduys-empfehluyen', *Marketing Zeitschrift Fur Forschung und Praxis*, vol. 17 (3), 162–76.

Hordes, M.W., Clancy, J.A. and Baddaley, J. (1995) 'A Primer for Global Start-ups', *Academy of Management Executive*, vol. 9 (2), 7–11.

Hout, T., Porter, M.E. and Rudden, E. (1982) 'How Global Companies Win Out', *Harvard Business Review*, vol. 60, September–October, 98–108.

Hu, Y.-S. (1992) 'Global or Stateless Corporations are National Firms with International Operations', *California Management Review*, 107–26.

Hunt, S. (1990) 'Truth in Marketing Theory and Research', *Journal of Marketing*, vol. 54 (July), 1–15.

Huntington, S. (1993) 'The Clash of Civilizations', *Foreign Affairs*, Summer, 22–49.

Ietto-Gillies, G. (1998) 'Different Conceptual Frameworks for the Assessment of the Degree of Internationalization: An Empirical Analysis of Various Indices for the Top 100 Transnational Corporations', *Transnational Corporations*, vol. 7 (1), 17–40.

Johanson, J. and Vahlne, J.E. (1990) 'The Mechanism of Internationalisation', *International Marketing Review*, vol. 7 (4), 11–24.

Johansson, J.K. and Yip, G.S. (1994) 'Exploiting Globalization Potential: U.S. and Japanese Strategies', *Strategic Management Journal*, vol. 15 (8), 579–601.

Jensen, O. (2001) 'Key-Account-Management', in H.H. Bauer and C. Homburg, (eds) *Schriftenreite Instituts fur Markforiendierk unternehmensführung*, University of Mannheim, Wiesbaden: Deutscher Universitiets verlag.)

Jöreskog, K.G. and Sörbom, D. (1996) *LISREL® 8: User's Reference Guide* (Chicago: Scientific Software International).

Kahn, J.S. (1995) *Culture, Multiculture, and Postculture* (San Francisco: Sage).

Kaiser, H.F. (1960) 'The Application of Electronic Computers to Factor Analysis', *Educational and Psychological Measurement*, vol. 20, 141–51.

Kaplan, A. (1964) *The Conduct of Inquiry* (Scranton, Penn.: Chandler).

Kearney, A.T. (2001) 'Measuring Globalization', *Foreign Policy*, January/February, 56–65.

Kieser, A. and Kubicek, H. (1992) *Organisation*, 3rd edn (Berlin: de Guyter).

Kim, W.C. and Hwang P. (1992) 'Global Strategy and Multinationals' Entry Mode Choice', *Journal of International Business Studies*, vol. 1, 29–53.

Kim, W.S. Lyn E.O. (1986) 'Excess Market Value, The Multinational Corporation, and Tobin's q-Ratio', *Journal of International Business Studies*, Spring, 119–25.

Kirkbride, P., Pinnington, P. and Ward, K. (2001) 'The State of Globalization Today', P. Kirkbride (eds), *Globalization: The External Pressures* (Chichester: John Wiley & Sons).

Kleinert, J., Schimmelpfennig, A., Schrader, K. and Stehn, J. (eds) (2000) *Globalisierung, Strukturwandel und Beschäftigung*; Kieler Studien 308 (Tübingen: Mohr).

Knoke, W. (1996) *Bold new world* (New York: Kodansha Intl).

Kobrin, S.J. (1991) 'An Empirical Analysis of the Determinants of Global Integration', *Strategic Management Journal*, vol. 12, 17–31.

Kobrin, S.J. (1994) 'Is There a Relationship Between a Geocentric Mind-set and Multinational Strategy?', *Journal of International Business Studies*, vol. 25 (3), 493–511.

Kogut, B. (1985) 'Designing Global Strategies: Profiting from Operational Flexibility', *Sloan management Review*, vol. 26(Fall), 27–38.

Kotabe, M. and Helsen, K. (2001) *Global Marketing Management*; 2nd edn (New York: John Wiley & Sons).

Kulessa, V., Frank, Ch. and Stangl, R. (1999) 'Internationales Key Account Management in der Investitionsgüterindustrie – am Beispiel IBM', *Thexis*, 4/1999, St Gallen, 18–25.

Kutschker, M. and Schmid, St (2002) *Internationales Management* (München, Wien: Oldenbourg).

Lecraw, D.J., Morrison, A.J. and Dunning, J.H. (1993) (eds) *Transnational Corporations and Business Strategy*, vol. 4 (London, New York: Routledge).

Leong, S.M. and Tan, C.T. (1993) 'Managing Across Borders: An Empirical Test of The Bartlett and Ghoshal [1989] Organizational Typology', *Journal of International Business Studies*, 24(3), 449–64.

Leontiades, J.C. (1985) *Multinational Corporate Strategy: Planning for World Markets* (Lexington, Mass.: Lexington Books).

Levitt, Th. (1983) 'The globalization of markets', *Harvard Business Review*, vol. 61 (3), 92–102.

Li, J. Guisinger St (1992) 'The Globalization of Service Multinationals in the "Triad" Regions: Japan, Western Europe and North America', *Journal of International Business Studies*, vol. 23 (4), 675–96.

Li, P.P. (1998) 'Towards a Geocentric Framework of Organizational Form: A Holistic, Dynamic and Paradoxical Approach', *Organization Studies*, vol. 19 (5) Winter.

Lorange, P., Morton, S. and Ghoshal, S. (1986) *Strategic Control* (St Paul, Minn.: West Publishing Co.).

Macharzina, K. (1992) *Unternehmensführung: Das Internationale Managementwissen; Konzepte – Methoden – Praxis* (Wiesbaden: Gabler).

Makhija, M.V., Kim, K. and Williamson S.D. (1997) 'Measuring Globalization of Industries Using a National Industry Approach: Empirical Evidence Across Five Countries and Over Time', *Journal of International Business Studies*, vol. 4, 679–710.

Malnight, T.W. (1996) 'The Transition from Decentralized to Network-based MNC Structures: An Evolutionary Perspective', *Journal of International Business Studies*, vol. 1, 43–65.

Martinez, J.I. and Jarillo, J.C. (1989) 'The Evolution of Research on Coordination Mechanisms in Multinational Corporations', *Journal of International Business Studies*, vol. 4, 489–514.

Martinez, J.I. and Jarillo, J.C. (1991) 'Coordination Demands of International Strategies', *Journal of International Business Studies*, vol. 3, 429–44.

Mauri, A.J. and Sambharya, R.B. (2001) 'The Impact of Global Integration on MNC Performance: Evidence from Global Industries', *International Business Review*, vol. 10, 441–54.

McDonald, M., Millman, T. and Rogers, B. (1997) 'Key Account Management: Theory, Practice and Challenges', *Journal of Marketing Management*, vol. 13, 737–57.

McMullin, E. (1984) 'A Case for Scientific Realism', in J. Leplin (eds) *Scientific Realism* (Berkeley Cal.: University of California).

Miles, M.B. and Huberman, A.M. (1994) *An Expanded Sourcebook – Qualitative Data Analysis*, 2nd edn (Thousand Oaks, London, New Delhi: Sage).

Millman, T.F. (1996) 'Global Key Account Management and Systems Selling', *International Business Review*, vol. 5 (6), 631–45.

Millman, T.F. (1999) 'From National Account Management to Global Account Management in Business-to-Business Markets', *Thexis*, vol. 4, 2–9.

Millman, T.F. and Wilson, K.J. (1995) 'From Key Account Selling to Key Account Management', *Journal of Marketing Practice: Applied Marketing Science*, vol. 1 (1), 9–21.

Millman, T.F. and Wilson, K.J. (1996) 'Developing Key Account Management Competencies', *Journal of Marketing Practice: Applied Marketing Science*, vol. 1 (1), 9–21.

Millman, T.F. and Wilson, L.J. (1998) 'Global Account Management: Reconciling Organisational Complexity and Cultural Diversity', *Proceedings of the 14th IMP Conference* (Finland: Turku University).

Montgomery, D.B. and Yip, G.S. (1999) 'Statistical Evidence on Global Account Management Programs', *Thexis*, vol. 4, 10–13.

Montgomery, D.B. and Yip, G.S. (2000) 'The Challenge of Global Customer Management', *Marketing Management*, vol. 9 (4) Winter (Chicago).

Morrison, A.J. (1990) *Strategies in Global Industries* (New York, Westport and London: Quorum Books).

Morrison, A.J. and Roth, K. (1992) 'A Taxonomy of Business-level Strategies in Global Industries', *Strategic Management Journal*, vol. 13 (6), 399–418.

Mosquet, X. (2002) 'The Genetic Code of Global Organizations: The Boston Consulting Group', in U. Krystek and E. Zur (eds), *Handbuch Internationalisierung*, 2nd edn (Berlin: Springer).

Naisbitt, J. (1994) *Global Paradox* (New York: William Morrow).

Nordström, K.A. (1990) *The Internationalization Process of the Firm – Searching for new Patterns and Explanations* (Stockholm School of Economics).

Neff, J. (2000) 'Rethinking Globalism', *Advertising Age*, vol. 71 (42), October.

Nicholas, St and Maitland E. (1998). *The Multinational Enterprise: New Research Agendas in International Business*, Discussion Paper No. 1., September, 3–23.

Nunnally, J. (1978) *Psychometric Theory*; 2nd edn (New York: McGraw-Hill).

Nunnenkamp, P., Gundlach, E. and Agarwal, J.P. (1994) *Globalisation of Production and Markets*, Kieler Studien (ed.), Institut für Weltwirtschaft an der Universität Kiel (Tübingen: Mohr).

OECD (1997) 'New Directions for Industrial Policy', *Policy Brief*, No. 3.

OECD (2000) *Globalisation: What Challenges and Opportunities for Governments?* Strategic Management and Policymaking; August.

Ohmae, K. (1990) *The Borderless World: Power and Strategy in the Global Marketplace* (London: Collins).

Parker, B. (1998) *Globalization and Business Practice: Managing Across Boundaries* (London: Sage).

Parvatiyar, A. (2001) *Global Customer Management – Process and Contingency Effects*, Speech at the International Symposium of Customer Relationship Management, 21 June 2001 (Linz: Johannes Kepler University).

Parvatiyar, A. and Gruen, Th. (2001) *Global Account Management Effectiveness: A Contingency Model*, Working Paper.

Payne, A. (1995) *Advances in Relationship Marketing*, The Cranfield Management Series (London: Kogan Page).

Penrose, E. (1959) *The Theory of Growth of the Firm* (New York: John Lacey).

Perkins, S.J. and Hendry, C. (2001) 'Global Champions: Who's Paying Attention?', *Thunderbird International Business Review*, vol. 43 (1), 53–75.

Perlitz, M. (1993) *Uni-Taschenbücher Betriebswirtschuyt*, no. 1560 (Stuttgart, Jena: Gustave Fischer).

Perlmutter, H. (1969) 'The Tortous Evolution of the Multinational Corporation', *Columbia Journal of World Business*, vol. 4 (1), 9–18.

Perry (2002) *Realism Rules OK: Scientific Paradigms and Case-based and Action Research in Marketing*, 1st International Workshop in Marketing and Management, Vienna, 8–14 April 2002.

Phatak, A.V. (1992) *International Dimensions of Management*, 3rd edn (Boston, Mass.: PWS-Kent).

Porter, M.E. (1986a) 'Changing Patterns of International Competition', *California Management Review*, vol. 28 (2), 9–40.

Porter, M.E. (1986b) *Competition in Global Industries* (Boston, Mass.: Harvard Business School Press).

Porter, M.E. (1993) 'Changing Patterns of International Competition', in D.J. Lecraw, A.J. Morrison and J.H. Dunning (eds), *Transnational Corporations: and Business Strategy*, 138–69.

Prahalad, C.K. and Doz, Y.L. (1987) *The Multinational Mission: Balancing Local Demands and Global Vision* (New York: The Free Press).

Prahalad, C.K. and Hamel, G. (1990) 'The Core Competence of the Corporation', *HBR*, vol. 68, May/June 1990, 79–91.

Radice, H. (1996) 'The Question of Globalization', *Competition and Change*, vol. 2 (1).

Ramaswamy, K., Kroeck, K.G. and Renforth, W. (1996) 'Measuring the Degree of Internationalization: A comment', *Journal of International Business Studies*, vol. 1, 167–77.

Rapp, R. (2000) 'Customer Relationship Management: Mehr als ein IT-Konzept', *Sales Profit*, 1 November 2000, 36–40.

Reich, R. (1991) *The Work of Nations: Preparing Ourselves for 21st Century Capitalism* (New York: Alfred Knopf).

Reina, P. Tulacz G.J. (2001) 'Global Firms Increase Their Local Presences', *ENR – Engineering News Record*, vol. 247 (4), 32–5.

Rhinesmith, S.H. (1993) *A Manager's Guide to Globalization* (Homewood, Ill.: Business One Irwin).

Robertson, R. (1995) Glocalization: Time-space and Homogeneity–Heterogeneity', in M. Featherstone, S. Lash and R. Robertson (eds), *Global Modernities* (London: Sage), 25–44.

Rugman, A.M. and Verbeke A. (1992) 'A Note on the Transnational Solution and the Transaction Cost Theory of Multinational Strategic Management', *Journal of International Business Studies*, vol. 4, 761–71.

Ruigrok, W. and Wagner, H. (2000) *Degree of Internationalization and Performance: An Organizational Learning Perspective*, Paper presented at the Academy of Management Conference, Toronto.

Schmidt, R. (1981) 'Zur Messung des Internationalisierungsgrades von Unternehmen', in W. Wacker, H. Haussmann and B. Kumar (eds), *Internationale Unternehmensführung* (Berlin: E. Schmidt) 57–70.

Scott, A.J. (1998) *Regions and the World Economy: The Coming Shape of Global Production, Competition and Political Order* (Oxford: University Press).

Senn, Ch. (1999) 'Implementing Global Account Management: A Process Oriented Approach', *Journal of Selling and Major Account Management*, vol. 1 (3) 10–19 (Southampton: The Sales Research Trust).

Senn, Ch. and Zeier, R. (2002) *Nine Key Enablers of Key Account Management*, SAMA Best Practice Forum at Zurich, 5 February 2002.

Sera, K. (1992) 'Corporate Globalization: A New Trend', *Academy of Management Executive*, vol. 6 (1), 89–96.

Shapiro, B. and Moriarty, R. (1982) *National Account Management: Emerging Insights* (Cambridge, MA: Marketing Science Institute).

Sheth, J.N. and Parvatiyar, A. (2001) 'The Antecedents and Consequences of Integrated Global Marketing', *International Marketing Review*, vol. 18 (1), 16–29.

Silverman, D. (2001) *Interpreting Qualitative Data: Methods for Analyzing Talk, Text and Interaction,* 2nd edn (London: Sage)

Steger, U. and Kummer, Ch. (2002) 'Auswirkungen der Globalisierung auf das strategische Management', in U. Krystek and E. Zur (eds), *Handbuch Internationalisierung;* 2nd edn (Berlin: Springer).

Stopford, J.M., Dunning, J.H. and Haberich, K.O. (1992) *Directory of Multinationals* (Basingstoke: Macmillan).

Storper, M. (1997) *The Regional World: Territorial Development in a Global Economy* (New York: The Guilford Press).

Strauss, A. and Corbin, J. (1998) *Basics of Qualitative Research: Techniques and Procedures for Developing Grounded Theory,* 2nd edn (London: Sage Publications).

Sullivan, D. (1994) 'Measuring the Degree of Internationalization of a Firm', *Journal of International Business Studies*, vol. 25 (2), 325–42.

Sullivan, J.L. and Feldman, S. (1979) *Multiple Indicators: An Introduction* (London: Sage).

Sullivan, L. (2001) 'Going Global Around the World, Everywhere the Same', *Ebn*, 1262 (May).

Swimme, B. (1984) *The Universe is a Green Dragon* (Santa Fe: Bear).

Taggart, J.H. (1992) 'Coordination versus Globalisation: The Multinational's Dilemma', *Multinational Business*, vol. 3, 1–12.

Talkington, A. (2001) 'Global Leadership: What Chemical Industry CEOs Think about Managing the Global Enterprise', *Chemical Market Reporter*, vol. 3, 34–8.

Thompson, J.D. (1967) *Organizations in Action* (New York: McGraw-Hill).

Tomlinson, J. (1991) *Cultural Imperialism* (MD: John Hopkins University Press).

Tully, S. (1994) 'Teens, the Most Global Market of All', *Fortune*, May 16, 90–6.

Turnbull, P.W. and Paliwoda, S.J. (1986) *Research in International Marketing* (London: Croom Helm).

UNCTAD (1998) *World Investment Report, 1998: Trends and Determinants* (Geneva: United Nations).

van den Berghe, D. (2001) *Measuring corporate internationalization and performance: A conceptualization and discussion of the indicators*, Paper presented at the Academy of Management Washington D.C.

Van Tulder, R. and Ruigrok, W. (1996) 'Regionalisation, Globalisation or Glocalisation: The Case of the World Car Industry, in M. Humbert (ed.), *The Impact of Globalisation on Europe's Firms and Industries* (London, New York: Pinter) 22–3.

Von Müller, A. (2002) 'Denkwerkzeuge für Global Player', in U. Krystek and E. Zur (eds), *Handbuch Internationalisierung*, 2nd edn (Berlin: Springer).

Wenig, A. (2000) *Globalisierung und die Zukunft der Sozialen Marktwirtschaft*, Volkswirtschaftliche Schriften, Heft 506 (Berlin: Duncker & Humblot).

Werani, Th. (1998) *Der Wert von Kooperativen Geschäftsbeziehungen in Industriellen Märkten: Bedeutung, Messung und Wirkungen* (Linz: Universitätsverlag Rudolf Trauner).

West, S.G., Finch, J.F. and Curran, P.J. (1995) 'Structural Equation Models with Nonnormal Variables: Problems and Remedies', in R.H. Hoyle (ed.), *Structural Equation Modeling: Concepts, Issues, and Applications* (Thousand Oaks: Sage), 56–75.

White, R.E. and Poynter, T.A. (1984) 'Strategies for Foreign-owned Subsidiaries in Canada; Business Quarterly, Summer, 59–69; cited in J.H. Taggart (1992) 'Coordination Versus Globalisation: The Multinational's Dilemma', *Multinational Business*, vol. 3, 2–3.

Wilson, K.J. (1999) 'Developing Global Account Management Programmes: Observations from a GAM Panel Presentation', *Thexis*, vol. 16 (4) St Gallen, 30 –5. (Universitët St Gallen).

Wilson, K., Millman, T., Weilbaker, D. and Croom, S. (2001) *Harnessing Global Potential: Insights Into Managing Customers Worldwide* (Chicago: Strategic Account Management Association).

Wilson, K., Speare, N. and Reese, S. (2002) *Successful Global Account Management*; Miller-Heiman (ed.) (London: Kogan Page).

Wright, R. (2001) 'Designing the Global Corporation', *Supply Management*, March, 36–7.

Wührer, G.A. (1995) *Internationale Allianz- und Kooperationsfähigkeit österreichischer Unternehmen: Beiträge zum Gestaltansatz als Beschreibungs- und Erklärungskonzept* (Linz: Rudolf Trauner Verlag).

Yip, G.S. (1992) *Total Global Strategy – Managing for Worldwide Competitive Advantage* (Englewood Cliffs: Prentice-Hall).

Yip, G.S. and Madsen, T. (1996) 'Global Account Management: The New Frontier in Relationship Marketing', *International Marketing Review*, vol. 13 (3), 24–42.

Zupancic, D. and Senn, Ch. (2000) *Global Account Management: Eine Bestandsaufnahme in Wissenschaft und Praxis*, Ch. Belz and T. Tomczak (eds) (St Gallen: Thexis).

Index